Swim & S

Aquatic Rhyme Ti.
Adventures!

By Emma Holden

An iconic photo of my swim school taken by Morley Photography in one of our early photo shoots.

All rights reserved. No part of this publication may be reproduced or transmitted in any form by any means, electronic, mechanical, including photocopy, recording or any information storage and revival system, without permission in writing from the author.
Copyright 2024 Emma Holden

First Edition 2024

Kindle Direct Publishing

Contents

Contents	3
Overview	5
About the Author	5
About The Book	8
History of Nursery Rhymes	10
Summary of Benefits and How to Enhance Learning	12
What are children actually learning?	12
Benefits of Songs in the pool - Positive Relations	14
Enhancing Positive Relationships in the pool	16
Benefits to Physical Development	19
Enhancing Physical Development	20
Benefits to Learning and Developing	22
The Brain and Music	23
Enhancing Learning and Developing	24
Benefits to a Unique Child	26
Enhancing A Unique Child	27
The Benefits of Songs in Learning to Swim	29
Enhancing Singing in swimming	30
Benefits to the Nervous System.	31
Swim & Sing in Practice	33
Conclusion	37
Case Studies	39
Study One,	39
Study Two	43

A Song A Week	46
Winter Theme (1, 2 and 3)	48
(also see weeks 51 and 52)	48
Food Theme (Weeks 4, 5, 6 and 7)	54
Forest Theme (Weeks 8,9,10 and 11)	62
Spring / Easter theme (Weeks 12, 13, 14, 15, and 16)	70
Space / Transport (Weeks 17, 18, 19, 20 and 21)	80
Oceans / Safety Theme (Weeks 22, 23, 24, and 25)	90
Summer Theme (Weeks 26, 27, 28, and 29)	98
Fairy Tales (Prince and Princesses) - (Weeks 30, 31, 32, and 33)	106
Busy Brains (Weeks 34, 35, 36, and 37)	114
Autumn - (Weeks 38, 39, 40, 41 and 42)	122
Celebrate themes (Weeks 43, 44, 45, and 46)	132
Strange Worlds Theme (Weeks 47, 48, 49, and 50)	142
Christmas Theme (part of winter) Weeks 51-52	152
Other celebration dates or ideas	156
Songs and Rhymes Ending Notes	157
Glossary of Holds	158
Index	163
Swim Skill Progression	163

Overview

About the Author

(Me with my second daughter in 2008)

I first knew I would work in the leisure industry around the age of 12 when whimsically reflecting on our future career with friends, I said "I want to have a 'fun' job, I'm going to work in a swimming pool all day!" This meandered over the next few years into 'I'm going to be a physiotherapist". Alas neither was to be for me straight away instead i embarked in office work which led me into accountancy. I always knew deep down this wasn't my purpose, so when I left to have my first child I began to train in holistic therapies. By the time my second Daughter was born I had moved into the world of babies and swimming!

This was 2008 and I have not looked back! Things were different back then and there wasn't the social support and knowledge sharing there is today so you could say I was, like many others of this time were, my own little pioneer, finding out what worked, what did not. Trying to bring in the holistic side of my learnings. It never resonated with me the regimental side of swimming nor the prescribed activities that were the norm of the time. Instead, I sought to find another way.

In 2016 I met with a wonderful play therapist with whom I discussed my idea of bringing imaginative play into the pool akin to dry side sensory classes that were all the rage. She provided me with 'sensory / treasure' baskets in the themes I had requested, and I went from there. These 'Aquatic Roleplay' classes were a huge hit, and learning went through the roof, the children were happy, there was rarely crying in my classes! Jackpot! There was nothing like it in the industry,

In 2018 I felt the urge to share these ideas with the world, and I did. Aquatic Roleplay Themes started and I began recording vlogs of the themes on YouTube. Written forms of these Lesson ideas went to swim instructors all over the world.

There have been many influences in my work in these latter years. Emie Kitson brought reflexes awareness into my radar through undertaking my Level 3 Diploma in baby and Preschool. Zara Peasland, and Kate Rigby satisfied my reflex itch in training me in Rhythmic Movement Training. Jo Wilson has been supportive, championing my work and inspiring me. The Swimming Teachers Association is amazing for allowing me to help raise standards in baby and preschool swimming through a series of free webinars that re-capped their wonderful teachings and allowing me to include my themed work and songs activities.

These webinars led to me winning the 'Henry Pike' award in 2023.

I became a swimming tutor in 2021, specialising in baby and preschool. Many people have influenced this tutoring aspect of my journey especially Rebecca Garwood who has supported my tutor journey from the very start.

I can honestly say it's my life passion and pleasure to help instructors find their passion and drive through play-based lessons whether it be through my tutoring or Facebook group.

But of course, my biggest influence is the tens of thousands of children that I have taught over years. I continue to be educated by my swimmers to this day, 4 days a week through my swim school Swim Play Academy.

I am very excited to share my research into song and rhyme in the pool with you and to share my 52 favourite songs and their progressive activities.

About The Book

Welcome to "Sing & Swim Aquatic Rhyme Time for Splash Adventures" a book designed to introduce you to 52 of my favourite nursery rhymes and songs. These songs will not only entertain your little swimmers but also enhance their swim and safety skills. It is the aim of this book to highlight the beneficial opportunity that song, rhyme and rhythm can bring to your swimming class. We will dive deep into the actions that accompany each song, allowing your swimmers to fully engage and importantly progress.

Throughout this book, we will also explore the fascinating history of nursery rhymes and songs. You will learn about their origins, the stories behind them, and how they have evolved over time. It's incredible to see how these timeless melodies have survived through the ages and how they continue to captivate children's hearts and minds. We will discuss the relevance and benefits of incorporating songs and rhymes into our modern-day swimming lessons including engaging case studies I have performed looking at the benefits of music in a learn to swim environment.

But that's not all, we will also explore how music ties in with the principles of the Early Years Scheme. These schemes are fundamental to a child's strands of development and include areas such as communication, physical development, emotional well-being, and more. By linking these themes to the role that songs and rhymes play in the swimming pool, we will discover how music can enhance and support a child's overall growth and learning process. Prepare to be amazed by the power of music!

Throughout the book I will also provide nuggets of information that can be used to help the parents and guardians of your swimmers to understand the often hidden benefits of songs and rhymes in a water based class. For example how music excites and helps fire and wire not just one part of the brain, but several! I understand parental communication is one of the top difficulties in teaching the early years to swim. With effective marketing, attention grabbing quotes and filling you knowledge on the benefits will not only help with this communication but will serve to enhance and grow your classes.

Each section details my top 5 enhancing tips when it comes to using song and rhyme in your learn to swim classes. These tips come from my heart and my experience since starting my swim teaching career back in early 2008. It is the gift that keeps giving, you will learn the songs and actions, the history, the benefits of, my top tips, and handy marketing phrases.

There's one thing for sure, this book will ignite your passion, knowledge on Songs, Rhymes and Rhythm in the pool and help you maintain and grow your customer base through its use.

Sayings (#6, #7) and Facts
Throughout this book you will see speech bubbles containing some great quotes and facts. I have researched and included these for you to use to inspire communication with your swimming families through newsletters, social media feeds etc. When parents see these snippets of information, it will hopefully pique their interest and encourage them to learn more about the benefits of nursery rhymes in swimming lessons. For example, you can mention how "Humpty Dumpty" promotes teamwork and cooperation through turn taking, or how "Row, Row, Row Your Boat" promotes Propulsive actions and the beginnings of regaining feet. These quotes and facts will not only inform parents but also show them how nursery rhymes can make a real difference in their child's swimming progress. Please see the reference section for their references.

History of Nursery Rhymes

The earliest written record of nursery rhymes dates back to as early as 1580 #1. These rhymes were passed down through generations and were initially composed for entertainment and educational purposes. It is theorised that the purpose of nursery rhymes is to teach young people about life lessons, but the earlier rhymes may have been targeted towards adults. Some nursery rhymes contain hidden meanings or references to political events, local celebrities, or historic occurrences. Nursery rhymes may have been sung even 2000+ years ago with it being widely believed that Romans would sing to their infants. #2

For example, let's take a closer look at the rhyme "Mary Mary quite contrary." Some speculate that this rhyme is about the villainous Queen Mary I, also known as Bloody Mary. The line "how does your garden grow?" could be a metaphor for how Mary's reign and religious policies affected the kingdom. Similarly, the rhyme "London Bridge is falling down" may have originated from the Great Fire of London in 1666. The bridge was damaged during the fire, and this rhyme could have been a way for people to remember the event.

Another interesting nursery rhyme is "baa baa black sheep." This rhyme might have been a commentary on the tax imposed on wool during mediaeval times. The line "one for the master, one for the dame, and one for the little boy who lives down the lane" could represent the different parties involved in the wool trade and how they benefited from it. Lastly, the story of Humpty Dumpty being a cannonball is often debated. Some argue that Humpty Dumpty refers to a cannon that was mounted on a wall during the English Civil War and was destroyed. #3

One thing is for sure. Children love to move, sing and recall these handy little rhymes with seeming ease.

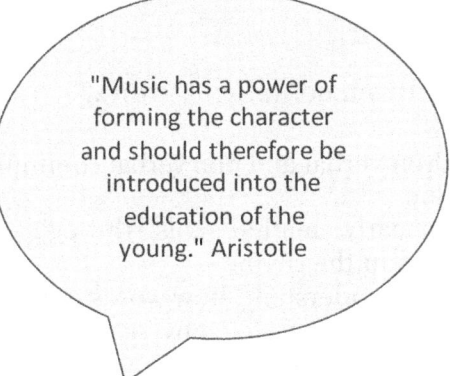

"Music has a power of forming the character and should therefore be introduced into the education of the young." Aristotle

Summary of Benefits and How to Enhance Learning

What are children actually learning?

- Children verbal and non verbal communication skills develop
- Learn early maths skills through counting and patterns in the rhyme
- Children understand how words are formed
- Enables children to copy actions and fire mirror neurons
- It boosts children's language and literacy skills - songs have a start, middle and end!
- Helps develop children's social skills and understanding of the world
- Children learn about different beats and rhythms
- Provides the opportunity for children to value and become confident learners.
- Creates a close relationship between adult and child

If adults are having fun, then their children are more likely to respond. Positive interactions like this in the pool are beneficial on not only a learning level but from attachment and bonding points of view.

How can adults assist in this learning in the pool

- Be confident
- Sing songs slowly and clearly - repeat the song several times
- Use a clear tone
- Use props or actions to support the songs
- Involve children - see how they interpret the song if allowed to make up actions - did they enjoy it?
- Lots of movement - when children move they learn

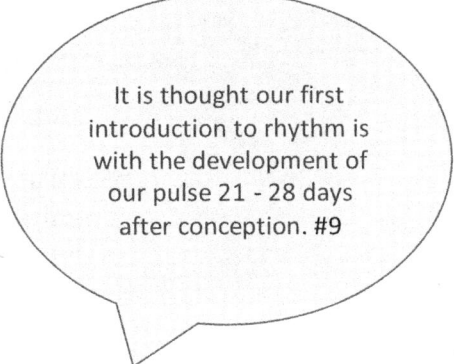

It is thought our first introduction to rhythm is with the development of our pulse 21 - 28 days after conception. #9

Benefits of Songs in the pool - Positive Relations

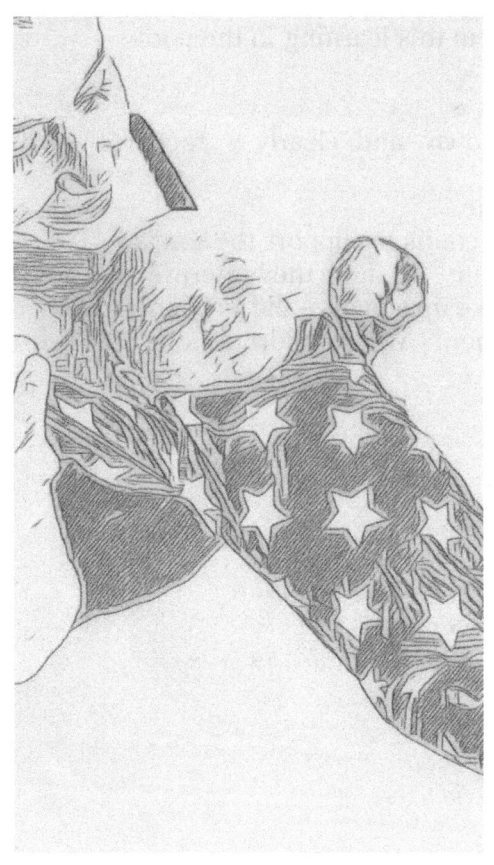

Let's take a moment to appreciate how and why songs and nursery rhymes benefit and contribute to building and enhancing positive relationships, not only in the pool but at home too. Positive relationships are one of the main themes of the Early Year Scheme, and many theorists believe they have a huge impact on a child's development. (Bowlby 1969) and (Mate 2019) both highlight the fundamental importance of a secure attachment for young people. Not just in the pool, but at home too which is why included in this programme are some bath time activity ideas for your swim families to enhance positive relations, and development on a whole.

This is where songs and nursery rhymes come in. They provide opportunities for children to bond with their caregivers and peers through shared experiences. Singing and reciting rhymes together create moments of connection and build trust. Whether it's a parent singing a lullaby to their baby, or a group of children singing and dancing together, these activities foster a sense of togetherness and belonging.

Furthermore, songs and nursery rhymes can also help children develop important social and emotional skills. They often convey messages of kindness, empathy, and cooperation, teaching children the value of positive relationships. For example, many nursery rhymes like "Row, Row, Row Your Boat" or "The Wheels on the Bus" involve actions and interactions that require cooperation and turn-taking. Through these activities, children learn to listen to others, take turns, and work together – all essential skills for building positive relationships.

Today, we will explore the importance of the adult and child pair forming a secure attachment through this special "Aquatic Rhyme Time." This time allows their energies to intertwine and synchronise, creating a strong bond between them. By engaging in two-way communication, trust and security are built, which are essential for the child to later feel confident in performing tasks in the pool. During Aquatic Rhyme Time, the child learns that their voice will be heard and valued, and they will have control over their actions.

Imagine a parent and child stepping into the pool together. As they start Aquatic Rhyme Time, they sing songs and perform actions in sync, mirroring one another's movements and words. Through this shared experience, the adult and child pair connect on a deeper level, creating a sense of trust and safety. The child knows that they can rely on their parents to listen to them and understand their needs. This secure attachment allows the child to feel comfortable in the water, knowing that they have a supportive and responsive adult by their side.

Let's consider an example to better understand the impact of Aquatic Rhyme Time. Imagine a child who is hesitant to try new things in the water. With their parent's encouragement, they engage in the activity and gradually become more comfortable. As they sing and move together, the child's confidence grows, and they start to explore their surroundings independently. This newfound trust and security built through Aquatic Rhyme Time enables the child to feel safe enough to venture out and try new tasks, such as floating on their back or finning their feet. By involving the child in the decision-making process and giving them control over their actions, the parent reinforces the idea that the child's voice matters, and they have agency in the water

Enhancing Positive Relationships in the pool

Building positive relationships in the pool is essential. It not only enhances the learning experience but also creates a safe and comfortable environment for children to develop their swimming skills. Aquatic rhyme time is a fantastic tool for fostering positive relationships in the pool. By incorporating fun and interactive rhymes into swimming lessons, instructors can help caregivers engage with children on a deeper level.

Here are my 5 top tips for building positive relationships through Aquatic rhyme time.

1. Get the children involved - example: For Jelly on the Plate - ask them which action they'd like, up and down or side to side? How should it be done? Should it be fast, slow, big, small? - this shows the child they are valued, that we trust them to make a decision, it allows them autonomy over their learning - it gives CONTROL to them.
2. Have them facing different ways, maybe one song facing and interacting with their caregiver and

another song facing and interacting with their peers through parallel, imitation or cooperative play.
3. Choose the tempo of the song according to the mood of the child or group. There are usually non-verbal (or verbal) cues that indicate when a child is needing a change in pace - maybe as the instructor you know it is time to climb out and know the children would benefit from a calmer song to bring energy down. Use this information to help the child adjust and engage.
4. Repetition - through repetition the children can gauge predictability so they can begin to understand social and emotional cues of all involved
5. Watch for disengagement. If a child is glazed over or distracted this could be as the song for whatever reason may be causing a freeze response ensure you enable their caregiver to take time to check in and hold space for the child to

It goes without saying that we should create a welcoming and inclusive atmosphere. It's important to make every child feel valued and accepted in the swimming class. Begin each lesson by greeting each child individually and using their names. This simple gesture helps to establish a personal connection from the start. During Aquatic rhyme time, encourage children to participate and make them feel like their contributions are important. This inclusive environment will empower children to express themselves and build trust with their swimming instructor.

Children thrive on positive energy, so bring your enthusiasm to every Aquatic Rhyme Time session. Show excitement when introducing the rhymes and engage with the children through animated facial expressions and body language. Your enthusiasm will rub off on the children and make the experience more enjoyable for everyone. Remember, the more fun they have, the more likely they are to develop a positive relationship with you as their swimming instructor which will stand you both in good stead when continuing in the learn to swim journey.

Every child is unique, and it's important to cater to their specific needs and preferences. Some children may be more shy or reserved, while others may be more outgoing. As a swimming instructor, take the time to understand each child's personality and adapt your approach accordingly. For example, if a child is particularly nervous, you can start with simpler rhymes and gradually build their confidence. By personalising Aquatic rhyme time, you are demonstrating to the children that you care about their individual journey and are invested in their progress.

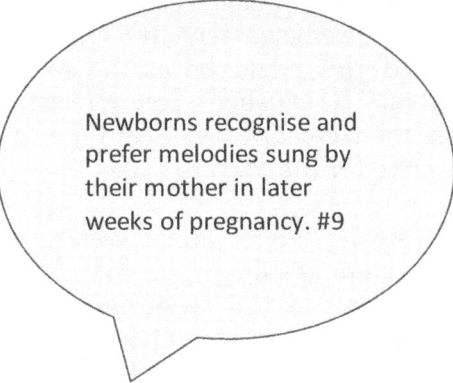

Newborns recognise and prefer melodies sung by their mother in later weeks of pregnancy. #9

Benefits to Physical Development

When children are born, they come into the world equipped with a self-fulfilling program that is ready to be played. This program is their innate ability to grow and develop, and it is fuelled by the power of play. Play is the operative word here. It is through play that children are able to fully unfold naturally and unlock their full potential. By giving children the opportunity and freedom to play, we are allowing them to tap into their own natural growth and development. Without this play-based approach, learning can be difficult and it becomes a struggle for children to progress in a linear manner.

One of the key elements that children possess from birth are their reflexes (Blomberg 2011). These reflexes are automatic responses that are built-in to help them navigate their early stages of life. For example, the rooting reflex helps babies find the source of nourishment when they are hungry, and the grasp reflex allows them to grip onto objects. These reflexes serve a purpose in their growth and development, and by allowing children to explore and play, we are providing them with the opportunity to stimulate and refine these reflexes. Through play, children are able to naturally and instinctively activate and develop these reflexes, which in turn will support their overall growth and development.

In addition to reflexes, children's senses play a crucial role in their development. When children engage in play, their senses are activated and in turn, they help to program the brain with the necessary information for healthy and successful development. For example, through sensory play, such as touching different textured materials or listening to different sounds, children are not only having fun, but they are also encoding important information in their brain. This information helps them to make sense of the world around them and to develop key skills, such as problem-solving, communication, and creativity. By providing children with opportunities for sensory play, we are giving them the chance to fully utilise their senses and enhance their learning and development.

With Aquatic Rhyme Time we aim to give the child time and space to unfold and grow into themselves organically. Through the songs children can explore movements that ordinarily they wouldn't. Fundamental movement skills can be heightened through repetition and practice. Children can not be expected to execute technical swimming skills without these foundations.

Enhancing Physical Development

There are countless opportunities to enhance physical development in the pool and it's sometimes more letting the child perform the action rather than doing the action for them that will lead to enhancement. Here are my Top 5 Tips for enhancing and developing physical development through songs and rhymes

1. Attainable - Ensure the actions are attainable for the age and developmental stage of the child – children learn best when the goal is achievable. This can be a balance but get it right and their progression will be easier.
2. Risk taking opportunities - Create a safe enabling environment for children to take risks.
3. Vary the movements - Keep moving, big movements, small movements, fast movements slow movements – mix the orientation of the actions

4. Focus - Have a focus skill and practise it in different ways though different songs and rhymes

5. Time - Ensure there is a long enough pause given in the class by yourself and the parent for the child to register and make the action independently.

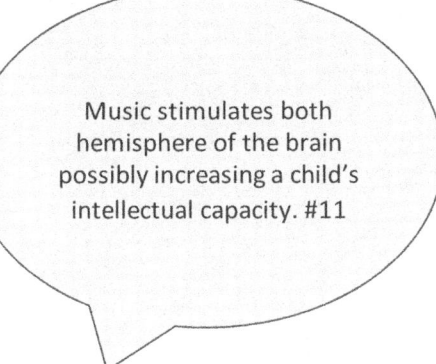

Music stimulates both hemisphere of the brain possibly increasing a child's intellectual capacity. #11

Benefits to Learning and Developing

Music has always been a powerful tool for learning and development, and this is especially true when it comes to

children's cognitive development. Songs and rhymes have been proven to have a significant impact on cognitive abilities, including literacy, maths, and language skills. When children listen to and participate in songs and rhymes, their brains are stimulated in ways that promote learning and enhance their cognitive abilities.

Let's start with literacy. Songs and rhymes help children develop phonological awareness, which is the ability to identify and manipulate individual sounds in words. For example, when children sing nursery rhymes that have repetitive sounds or rhyming words, such as "Twinkle, Twinkle, Little Star," they learn to recognise and differentiate sounds. This helps them with letter recognition, spelling, and reading comprehension. Moreover, the rhythm and melody in songs and rhymes help children remember the words and phrases more easily, boosting their overall literacy skills.

In addition to literacy, songs and rhymes also have a positive impact on children's maths skills. Many nursery rhymes incorporate counting and numerical concepts, such as "One,

Two, Buckle My Shoe" or "Five Little Ducks". These rhymes introduce children to numbers and counting in a fun and engaging way. By singing and reciting these rhymes, children develop a strong foundation for numerical understanding and arithmetic. They also improve their problem-solving skills, as they learn to follow sequences and patterns within the songs and rhymes.

Last but certainly not least, songs and rhymes are beneficial for language development. When children sing or recite rhymes, they are exposed to a rich vocabulary and a variety of sentence structures. This exposure helps expand their language skills and enhances their ability to express themselves orally. Moreover, the repetitive nature of many songs and rhymes allows children to practise and reinforce language concepts, such as sentence structure and grammar. As a result, children who regularly engage in singing and reciting rhymes have better language skills and are more confident communicators.

The Brain and Music

There have been many studies into how music, rhythm, and songs affect the brain. It is only now becoming understood that music affects many parts of the brain in different ways. One area that is heavily impacted by music is the emotional centre of the brain, known as the amygdala. When we listen to music, it can evoke strong emotions and elicit memories associated with certain songs or melodies. For example, a song that was popular during a happy time in our lives may bring back those feelings when we hear it again. Similarly, a song that was playing during a sad or difficult time may cause us to feel those emotions all over again. This connection between music and emotions is incredibly powerful and can be harnessed for therapeutic purposes, such as music therapy for individuals with psychological or emotional issues.

In addition to influencing our emotions, music also affects the reward centre of the brain, which is responsible for releasing dopamine, a neurotransmitter associated with pleasure and motivation. When we listen to music that we enjoy, our brains release dopamine, giving us a sense of pleasure and reward. This is why we often experience a sense of joy or euphoria when listening to our favourite songs or attending live concerts. Music can also act as a natural painkiller, as the release of dopamine can help reduce the perception of pain. This has led to the use of music therapy in medical settings, particularly for individuals experiencing chronic pain or undergoing invasive procedures.

Furthermore, music has been found to enhance cognitive function and improve certain mental processes. Research has shown that listening to classical music, particularly compositions by Mozart, can temporarily boost spatial-temporal reasoning skills, which are important for tasks such as problem-solving and mathematical reasoning. This phenomenon, known as the "Mozart effect," has led to the belief that listening to classical music can make individuals smarter. While the long-term effects of the Mozart effect are still debated, it is clear that music has the ability to engage and stimulate the brain in unique ways. This is why incorporating music into educational settings, such as using songs to teach children multiplication tables or foreign languages, can be highly effective in promoting learning and retention.

Enhancing Learning and Developing

It is said if a child is moving they are learning (#4), Rhythm is a movement that activates the memory sores and I believe it helps children with those ahhh moments. It helps them experiment and explore their ideas. I have countless tips I have discovered whilst teaching thousands of children to swim regarding all facets of learning but these are my top 5.

1. Choice this is my biggest tip – allow the child to choose, choose how they will do an action for example big or small or for example which animal in a song they will sing or how we should end a song. Choice leads to better connections.

2. Connections - Help them understand their choice better – This is a double whammy as they will feel valued and respected, enhance communication but also cement learning. For example 'praise the choice and ask them why they chose it'
3. Repeat – Repeat the song in conversational ways as well as singing – For example 'Did you like rowing through the trees? Was it a surprise when we sang if you see the monkeys kick and paddle please?' 'You kicked really well can you show me again or what do monkeys say? Can you sway like a tree.'
4. Focus – Have a focus throughout the songs for example the focus may be speed or size and bring attention to those elements afterwards.
5. Time – Allow time for a child to digest and learn from the song and its actions including pauses to see if they will initiate actions and words for themselves.

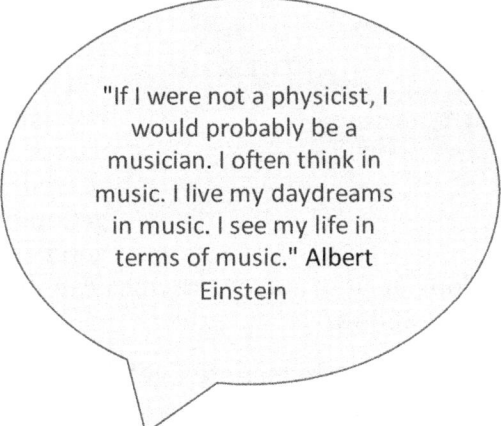

"If I were not a physicist, I would probably be a musician. I often think in music. I live my daydreams in music. I see my life in terms of music." **Albert Einstein**

Benefits to a Unique Child

Research has shown that nursery rhymes play a crucial role in a child's development and can help them become unique individuals. Nursery rhymes are not just fun and entertaining but also provide numerous benefits that contribute to a child's overall growth and happiness. These timeless melodies and catchy verses have been passed down through generations, and for a good reason. Let's take a closer look at how nursery rhymes can empower children to stand out and thrive.

Moreover, nursery rhymes offer children a sense of creativity and imagination. They often use vivid imagery and nonsensical elements that spark a child's curiosity and encourage them to think outside the box. For example, "Hey Diddle Diddle" portrays a cat playing the fiddle and a cow jumping over the moon. Such fantastical scenarios capture a child's imagination, fuelling their capacity to think beyond the boundaries of reality. By engaging with nursery rhymes, children learn to embrace their unique perspectives, foster creativity, and develop their own imaginative worlds.

Being unique can lead to better prospects and lifelong happiness. Many people strive to fit in with the crowd, believing that conformity is the key to success. However, this mindset often leads to a lack of fulfilment and missed opportunities. Embracing our individuality can set us apart from others in a positive way and open doors to new opportunities. When we let go of societal expectations and embrace our unique qualities, we become more authentic and attract people who appreciate us for who we truly are. In this lesson, we will explore the benefits of being unique and how it can lead to a more fulfilling life.

One of the greatest advantages of being unique is the ability to stand out in a crowd. When we dare to be different, we catch the attention of others and leave a lasting impression. Whether it's in a job interview, social setting, or networking event, being unique can give us a competitive edge. Employers are looking for individuals who bring fresh perspectives and innovation to the table. By showcasing our unique qualities and experiences, we can demonstrate our value and make a memorable impression. Likewise, in our personal lives, being unique can attract like-minded individuals who appreciate our quirks and embrace our individuality.

Being unique can lead to lifelong happiness. When we embrace our true selves and let go of the need for validation from others, we free ourselves from the constraints of societal pressures. This allows us to pursue our passions and interests without fear of judgement or rejection. By following our own path, we can create a life that aligns with our values and brings us joy. Additionally, being unique empowers us to define success on our terms rather than relying on external measures. When we are true to ourselves, we are more likely to find fulfilment and happiness in our achievements, no matter how big or small.

Enhancing A Unique Child

"Today you are You, that is truer than true. There is no one alive who is Youer than You." Dr Seuss,

This is one of my favourite Dr Seuss quotes! He knew the importance of uniqueness and pioneered to enhance it through rhythm and rhyme. We too have a unique opportunity to allow children to grow and flourish into individuals in all senses of the word.

Here are my top 5 tips.

1. Choice – As with learning and developing this is my biggest tip. Ensure the child has choice, choice in how to explore the actions and song – do they prefer to face parents or peers? Do they wish to watch or join in? How loud do they want to sing?
2. Opinions – Ask them! Show your mutual value and respect through seeking opinions
3. Imitation – Choose songs that allow expression through imitation, I find many personalities shine when choice and opinion are combined through imitation.
4. Discourage comparisons - Help parents acknowledge and accept that their child's personality may differ from theirs and their peers - Children will develop in their own way and rate (#5)
5. Space – Create an environment that allows for freedom of expression, creativity such as playing a game alongside a song with an openly creative objective .

The Benefits of Songs in Learning to Swim

Learning to swim can be a daunting task for many children. The fear of water, the unfamiliarity of the swimming pool, and the physical demands of swimming can all make it challenging to learn this important life skill. However, one effective and enjoyable way to aid in the process of learning to swim is through the use of nursery rhymes. Nursery rhymes provide numerous benefits that can help children become more comfortable and confident in the water.

Firstly, nursery rhymes can help create a positive association with swimming. Singing familiar nursery rhymes, such as "Row, Row, Row Your Boat" or "The Itsy Bitsy Spider," while in the water can help make swimming a fun and enjoyable experience. These songs can serve as a distraction from any anxieties or fears associated with swimming, and can create a sense of excitement and anticipation. By using nursery rhymes as a tool, children can develop a positive attitude towards swimming, making the learning process more enjoyable.

In addition to creating a positive association, nursery rhymes can also serve as a valuable teaching tool. Many nursery rhymes have actions or movements associated with them, such as "Twinkle, Twinkle, Little Star" with its hand motions. These actions can be adapted to suit the movements and skills needed for swimming. For example, using the actions from "The Wheels on the Bus" can help children practise paddling their arms in the water. By incorporating these movements into swimming lessons, children can develop their swimming skills while engaging with familiar and enjoyable nursery rhymes.

Enhancing Singing in swimming

Here are my top tips

1. Ensure the actions are age appropriate no child wishes to fail, they will gain far more self esteem if the action is achievable.
2. Is the song familiar ? Familiar songs will give the parents more confidence and make it more likely a child will join in.
3. Sing each song three times or songs with four or five verses once or twice, Explaining the holds and actions of the song, demonstrating and checking understanding, Then add the song pausing after the first verse to give praise, corrections, adaptations, progressions, then sing the remaining rounds pausing in between for praise and corrections if necessary.
4. Purposeful progressions – Have a clear progression path in your mind to help guide the swimmers up and down this will boost their confidence and grow their ability.
5. Get Feedback from the pairs – this will help you adapt and grow.

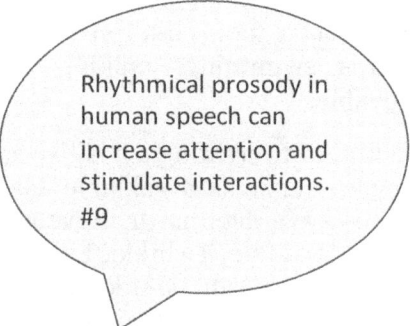

Rhythmical prosody in human speech can increase attention and stimulate interactions.
#9

Benefits to the Nervous System.

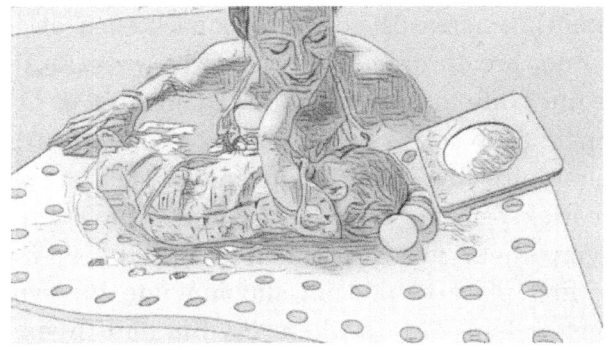

Whilst I am no expert and what I write here is purely from my experience and unguided research I can say that my understanding is as follows: In brief our Nervous system comprises the central nervous system and the peripheral nervous system. The peripheral nervous system gathers information through a network of nerves that gains their information from the senses (sight, sound, smell, touch, taste, vestibular). This all passes into the brain for processing allowing us to understand what is happening outside of our body and how our body is and effects in that world around us (proprioception). If we know how to 'listen' it also tells us what's happening inside our body (interoception) and what we perceive to be happening inside another person's body. Our brains are so amazing that they use this nervous system to look for tiny indications on people's faces, such as pupil dilation or a slight lift in the eyebrow for example to determine if that person is a threat or not (ventral vagal system). This makes it so important that you are genuinely enjoying the song and that the parents are comfortable. This coupled with felt muscular tension these children are typically hard wired to read the signs.

The peripheral nervous system can be further broken down into the Parasympathetic system (Rest and digest) and the Sympathetic nervous system (fight flight freeze). When Our amygdala sounds the alarm and activates the sympathetic nervous system, it turns down the cortex (the logical parts of the brain) , increases stress responses such as increased heart rate, breathing changes, even being sick. Adrenaline floods our body for a boost of energy making us jittery - all to prepare us to battle, flee or hide from the perceived threat. To help return to a normal state and re-open the shutters to the cortex so to speak, we need to activate the parasympathetic nervous system or indeed keep it activated in the first place to prevent slipping into the sympathetic nervous system. This is where rhythm and rhyme come in and scream to the amygdala actually, I'm safe!

Ideas and top tips to help activate the parasympathetic include drumming, especially repeating patterns.

- Rhythmic moves, and sways slowly awaken the vestibular sense and bring the body back into homeostasis. Try Clap clap splash, even better if you can make a repeating pattern that involves the left, right and centre of the midline for example right hand splash, left hand splash, clap.
- Humming this calms breathing and stimulated the vagal nerve to help with parasympathetic arousal - try humming a song without using words
- Bubbles as the humming works, so does bubbles! Good job we are in the water!

Swim & Sing in Practice

Whether you wish to run a session full of songs, rhyme and rhythm or simply wish for a section of aquatic rhyme time during a lesson the songs in this programme are sure to be loved by your swimmers and their caregivers.

Aquatic Rhyme Time is an engaging approach to enhancing swimming lessons that offers a host of benefits for both children and instructors. One of the key advantages of running a full Aquatic Rhyme Time lesson is that it allows for mixed ages in a group setting. This means that children of different ages and abilities can participate in the same class, singing the same song, and offering differing actions. This not only promotes inclusivity and a sense of community but also allows for peer learning and support. Younger children can learn from and be inspired by the older ones, while the older ones can develop leadership skills by modelling and guiding their younger peers.

In addition to its inclusive nature, Aquatic Rhyme Time is also a great option for classes that may not suit the majority of students due to limited pool time. For example, if a swim school only has access to the pool at lunchtimes or school run pick up time. Aquatic Rhyme Time can open up that awkward time to a more diverse range of adult and child pairs, serving as a valuable alternative that fills up the class time effectively. By focusing on singing, movement, and fun, the class becomes an opportunity for children to simply enjoy being in the water, building water confidence, and developing a positive association with swimming.

It is great that Aquatic Rhyme Time can be seamlessly integrated into swimming lessons as a complementary activity. Traditional swimming lessons often prioritise teaching specific techniques, which can sometimes feel daunting or rigid for young learners. By incorporating singing and rhymes into the lesson, instructors can help alleviate any pressure to perform or achieve certain outcomes. Instead, the children can grow and unfold in their own time, guided by the rhythm and joy of the aquatic rhymes. This approach not only enhances the overall swimming experience but also encourages creativity, self-expression, and a love for the water.

This program is designed to complement my "Aquatic Roleplay Themes". I am working on a book with a theme a month to coincide with this book. In the book to follow, we will dive into various topics, such as "Strange Worlds". We will explore different progressive games that fit within this theme and show you how to use these games to create engaging Aquatic Roleplays Themes or simply have fun exploring them in your swim school. By breaking down the topic and spreading it over a month, children will have the opportunity to grasp the concept and repeat games they love. Taking the learning fun from the pool into their homes. I have chosen the topics or 'themes' to coincide with important dates in the calendar. It is my hope that therefore these chosen topics will also coincide with topics that the children may be exploring in their playgroups, nurseries and pre schools.

Imagine taking your little swimmers to another dimension where they encounter magical creatures, lost worlds, and mysterious landscapes. With games like "Dinosaur Eggs" or "who's the wicked witch of the west", your students will have a blast exploring these strange worlds all the while practising and honing their swimming skills! These games are not only fun but also help improve their confidence in the water and develop important motor skills and make a fantastical addition to Aquatic Rhyme Time.

One example of a game within another theme "Oceans" is a kind of "Sea Creature Charade". In this game, you can ask the children to pick a sea creature and act it out while their friends guess what they are pretending to be, or we ask their caregiver to act it out. This is a two prongs approach; one they are independent whilst their caregiver completes the task and secondly they are learning by imitation. This game encourages creativity, imagination, and teamwork. Another game that fits well within this theme is "Treasure Dive". Hide objects at the bottom of the pool and challenge the children to retrieve them. This game promotes diving skills, breath control, and problem-solving as they search for the hidden treasures.

Watch out for news on the release of this book

My Overall tips for applying Aquatic Rhyme Time in practice is that children will not care if your voice isn't up to scratch! What they do care about is that you are present and that they are enjoying the song.

Here are my 5 top tips.

1. Practise the songs prior to the pool session – explore possibilities on how it can be adapted to suit your swimmers' individual needs, so you have some ideas ready.
2. Know that children won't care if your voice isn't up to perfect standards. What matters to them is that you and their caregiver are present and the enjoyment of the song. Have FUN together. Be truly present.
3. Sing each song 3 times, Explain the song and its actions (or allow children to), set the safe organisation and practise the holds and moves without the song. Then add the song, after 1st attempt give any corrections, progressions, or provoke thought from the child on how to improve. Then repeat twice pausing for praise and any enhancements between. Afterwards ask for feedback and give feedback.

4. Space and time – create space and time for the children to be as independent as possible and adapt holds and progressions to suit the individual.
5. Keep a focus on the songs you will sing in a session, ie make sure they allow choice but also point to a skill, be it swimming, learning and developing, movement skills, unique child, positive relations

> "A bird does not sing because it has an answer. It sings because it has a song." A Chinese proverb
>
> "Music expresses that which cannot be put into words." Victor Hugo

Conclusion

By now, you have learned and understand the positive impact Songs, Nursery rhymes, rhythm, rhyme and music can have on swimming lessons. Nursery rhymes are not only fun and engaging for children, but they also serve as a valuable teaching tool. Incorporating nursery rhymes into your lessons we have learnt can enhance learning, build confidence, and create a positive atmosphere in the pool.

It is now our duty to create an environment that is rich in opportunity for the children to explore and grow. enabling them to reach their fullest potential.

Nursery rhymes have a rich history dating back centuries. They have been passed down from generation to generation and have become ingrained in our culture. By sharing this knowledge with parents, you can help them understand the importance of nursery rhymes in your swimming lessons. It is not just about singing and having fun; it is about tapping into a centuries-old tradition that brings joy and learning to their child's swimming experience.

I am thrilled to have had the opportunity to share this book with you.

If you have any questions, suggestions, or if you simply want to connect, don't hesitate to reach out to me. You can visit www.swimplay.co.uk/aquatic-roleplay-themes for more information and to get in touch. I am here to support you and provide any additional resources, or ideas that can enhance your Aquatic Rhyme Time experience. Together, let's make learning a joyous and memorable adventure!

Please join my facebook group 'Aquatic themes top tips' or visit my dedicated page www.swimplay.co.uk/aquatic-rolepay-themes for further publications, CPDs and tutoring services.

Thank you!

> "Music is a more potent instrument than any other for education, because rhythm and harmony find their way into the inward places of the soul." – Plato

> According to the National Institute on Deafness and Other Communication Disorders (NIDCD) in the US, a child's first three years of life is the most intensive period for acquiring speech and language skills #8

Case Studies

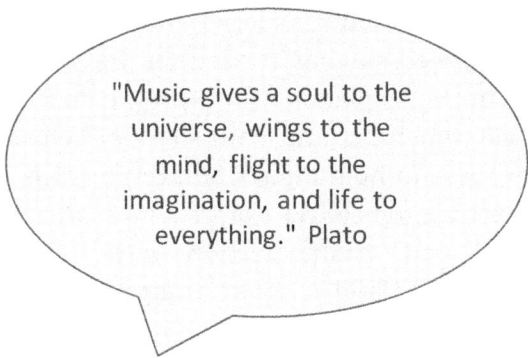

"Music gives a soul to the universe, wings to the mind, flight to the imagination, and life to everything." Plato

Here are 2 case studies from my personal swimming classes.

Study One,

Offering activities that will increase a child's independence will help them to grow in confidence both physically and cognitively allowing their self esteem to grow. This will in turn improve their development. They must be allowed the freedom to have a go in a safe environment independent of help. Maria Montessori says "We must clearly understand that when we give the child freedom and independence, we are giving freedom to a worker already braced for action, who cannot live without working and being active." (Montessori 2009 p91.)

Child A is 4 years old, large for his age and due to start primary school in September. He is an only child with older parents who have a busy hard working lifestyle. Swimming lessons previously have not been successful. There are no known medical or behavioural issues.

Week 1

Child A clung to mum in the pool and appeared to have no balance or strength. He was willing to listen and looked willing to be there. My lesson aim was to use songs and rhymes to help him become more independent and gain control of his movements. We discussed buoyancy and how he could help himself counteract it by learning to regain his feet independently. Step one was to hold the pool ladder and allow his legs to float up and then regain feet. We agreed singing 'the legs in the pool float up and down 6 times', explaining the more we do it the more the brain will remember and learn so it can help us next time. Step two was to hold mum's hand. We again agreed on 6 tries this time to baa baa black sheep as this was Child As Choice. I had a conversation with mum about the importance of Child A trying things independently. We reminded mum to let him hold on at the wall independently and walk about independently. Child A was quite cumbersome and un-agile, but he looked happy and mum held back from helping.

Week 2

This week child A remembered we liked it when he tried on his own and asked to be left to climb in independently and a bit unbalanced. He managed to walk across the pool, immediately took hold of the ladder and started the regain feet exercise singing baba baa black sheep without being asked. He lacks the coordination and balance to try without holding on and gets upset when his face becomes wet. We pause and discuss ways he can 'deal' with this independently (the 1 wipe only method), he then proceeds to splash his own face and use the 1 wipe method – we sing this is the way we wash our face. It was our spring week and he enjoyed collecting seeds (with help of mum for balance and propulsion), with the aid of singing when we were in the pool, we picked the seeds. He managed on the first attempt with only the song as guidance.

Week 3

This is our maths week and child A liked counting songs, guessing and making independent decisions, this led to a how many games for regaining feet, how many kicks before regaining feet, how many ear dips before regaining feet. Child A had also been practising splashing his face at home and using the 1 wipe method. I set a new challenge splash face count to... he offered 5 then wiped. We sang when we are in the pool. We wash our face 1, 2, 3, 4, 5 all day long. I can see him relaxing and feeling in control and being very proud of himself. Self-esteem is crucial for health brain development and progression

Week 4

This was a stand back! I am getting in alone! I am going to kick my legs by myself, hold on by myself, splash my face myself kind of lesson. It was Star Wars week so we talked about how to kick your legs and toes like lightsabers brushing past each other. He proceeded to include this for our actions to 3 jedi knights in an x wing fighter flew around the stars one day, saying I'm doing it I'm doing it! He also wanted to show me how he could now wet his face and not wipe at all!

Week 5

Child A got in independently. We enjoyed a great lesson together where we worked on a little rotation and direction and getting some propulsive actions letting child A try again where needed and praising the effort, reminding him that the brain sometimes needs to try different pieces before it can complete the jigsaw and remember for next time. (Montessori, M (2009)). Today we did more swimming than walking and he seems more confident and is starting to be able to propel himself independently. He climbed out independently for Humpty Dumpty song jumping in with only 1 hand for confidence.

Week 6

Child A arrived undressed himself, fully following any instructions given without hesitation, we followed his lead in activities but guided the choices to fit in with my plan to build on independence, balance and propulsion. Child A now seeks challenges and enjoys trying.

Conclusion

Childs A's swimming progression has improved significantly through giving him the tools he needs to be confident to give things a go by himself. The songs and Rhymes have provided a veil for Child A to feel secure behind whilst exploring his independence. Lessons have had a huge impact on Childs as self-esteem he is happier in most aspects at home and mum says does far more tasks independently whilst singing through choice and his gross motor skills over all have improved. I feel we still have a way to go to improve his physicality but, I truly agree we will get there quicker now his independence is enabled.

> Newborns up to 8 weeks have been known to accelerate synchronised sucking when familiar melodies were played #9

Study Two

Child B, 16 months of age had a typical birth, living with both parents, Mum is a stay at home mum.

Child B started with me at 14 months after attending swimming lessons with another provider since the age of 4 months. They didn't feel swimming lessons to date have been beneficial as after a great few months progress had stopped, and B has become upset and 'clingy'. It is my theory that potentially Child B's communication cues have been missed, ignored or misunderstood which has resulted in a lack of trust, attachment and enjoyment. (Bowlby 1969) It is my intention to re-build the pair's attachment and trust to help bring enjoyment back. I will do this through 2 way communication and music.

Week 1

B is visibly upset, body language is rigid and B is trying to fight away from the pool. I ask mum not to get in but to sit away from the pool edge and just join in from the poolside. We sing a variety of songs and rhymes with actions too and after about 10 mins Child B joins in from the side and relaxes. Mum wants to get in now, I tell her only if B consents. She does not, so they continue to sit poolside until the end of the lesson.

Week 2

I ask mum to sit poolside again but this time with her feet in the water and to only get in if B consents willingly. Surprisingly after the welcome song, B happily sits on the poolside while mum swivels in and they join the singing. We move on to drumming the water with our hands and B clings to mum again but she looks curiously on. No crying this lesson but no active participation.

Week 3

I ask mum to sit poolside again until B consent to getting in. B consents straightaway. We keep the routine the same, welcome song, some rhythmic splashing and rhythmic bubbles. B joins in later with the splashing and I ask mum to keep her really close but turn her around to face away. We continue with songs and propulsive activities – when we move away from the circle to widths B gets upset and we turn her to face mum. I suggest asking her if she wants to get out or stop for a cuddle and watch – she's opts to get out.

Week 4

B is happy, but again when we move to widths or have mat time B is visibly upset. They cuddle and I encourage eye contact and mirroring. I asked mum why she thinks this is and she thought it was potentially because previous classes would include submersions during these activities. We sing more songs and ensure we keep checking to see if she's happy and if she wants to join in, how close she wants to be, does she want to splash etc. She seems to love the songs and joins in happily.

Week 5

B joins in throughout the class, except mat work; however she was happy to hold the mat for others and join in with the songs we added to the activity.

Week 6

B got on the mat climbing up onto her belly and laying on it we sang row row and gently moved it back and forth after 1 verse B wiggled off into mum's arms. This was a huge risk for her. The rest of the lesson went well.

Conclusion

Adding an activity B deemed as safe and was happy she would be respected brought her out of her shell and allowed her to start forming trust again with mum and myself. Watching her peers being listened to and joining in I also feel would have helped. I think when she's realised that we would listen and wait for her to be ready it has given her confidence. Without the songs to calm her nervous system I feel we would still be on poolside waiting, songs are familiar and the actions are nourishing to the body to shift into a parasympathetic nervous state and movements to help release and express pent up emotion (Baxter 2022). It is also allowing mum and child to re connect and build trust in an activity together.

> The English language has more than forty sounds but only twenty-six letters, so a child needs to learn not just letters but phonemes too. #10

A Song A Week

Included in this section are a selection of 52 songs that can be used in adult and child swimming classes, a brand new song per week for a whole year!

They are ordered to start in January and run though to the year end. These engaging fun songs have been tried and tested throughout my career and are amongst my favourite rhymes and songs to help make learning fun in the pool. Specifically chosen, these 52 songs also coincide and compliment the predetermined 12 monthly themes listed.

A further book is in the making to detail in full the 12 Aquatic Roleplays Themes, games and activities relating to these topics: giving you a whole year of ideas to plan your lessons to.

Please see the glossary of holds to identify the holds suggested, however it is important that you ensure that any activity, or hold is at the comfort of the individual therefor please adapt where you see fit.

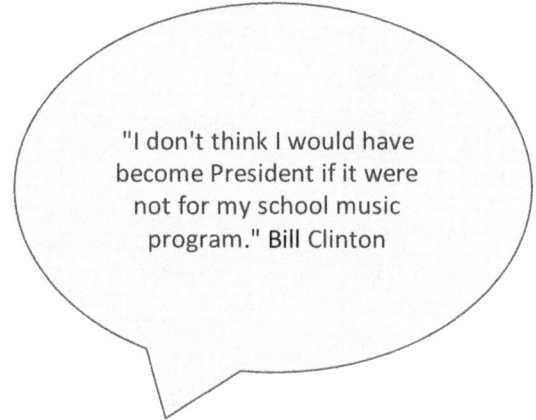

"I don't think I would have become President if it were not for my school music program." Bill Clinton

Enjoy

Winter Theme (1, 2 and 3)

(also see weeks 51 and 52)

Notable Dates: Christmas, Hanukkah, Winter Solstice, National Ice Day.

Snowflakes and Icicles
(Mary had a little lamb)

Snowflakes drift so softly to the ground,
softly to the ground, softly to the ground,
Snowflakes drift so softly to the ground,
Floating round and around.

Icicles are thin and long,
Thin and long, thin and long
Icicles are thin and long,
Jump up/kiss me while we Sing this Song

Activities

2-6m: [Cradle hold] soft swaying to the rhythm progressing to [dynamic back float hold] with a kiss on jump. Also could add touch with pitter patter fingers for snowflakes and long strokes for icicles (with consent)

6-12m [Yolk hold] soft swaying to rhythm progressing to a [Forward Surf] snaking action, or an open safety rotation

1-2yrs [Seat hold] – Seat lifts with swaying up and down progressing to popping hands in air. With a turntable rotation for snowflakes and a jump up for icicles.

2-4ys [Standing hold] – balancing being lifted up and down finally into a guided turntable rotation progressing to with consent a lap jump into an independent turntable rotation.

General/Tips: Make the actions and sway to the rhythm, starting high and swaying downwards, then make your body like a point and jump up at the end. Watch for reactions to actions and adapt where needed, some kids will love the fast ones and want more other may not. Gestures to fire mirror neurons and add visuals to word meanings. Mindful breathing, and breath in soft warm 2..3...4 and breath out all the bitter coldness 2...3...4)

Progression trail: Turntable Rotation - Balance

Snowman
(Little Teapot)

I'm a little snowman round and fat

I've got a woolly scarf and a fluffy bobble hat

When the snow is falling, come out and play

You can make a snow man today.

Activities:

2-6m: [Yolk Hold] – Sway to rhythm – Adult and child turn 360 together for round and fat. Parent Face dips (ensuring parent emphasises closed mouth) for coming out and play.

6-12m: As above – invite the infant to copy face dip by adding a signal and pause at the end to give the opportunity IF infant chooses.

1-2yrs: As above but only turning the infant 360 for round and fat. Parents dip their hair back for hat and face in for come out and play. Giving opportunities for children to try independently at the end.

2-4yrs: Progress to independent 360s, Independent washing hair for hat, popping face in for come out and play in a flip flop rotation style finishing with a snowman float and regaining feet.

General/Tips: We also like to do round arms to draw the snowman in the water, then touch our neck and our head (body recognition). We throw the water in the air for the snow is falling and rhythmically tap or blow bubbles into the water for the last line.

Progression Trail: Turntable Rotation and Vertical Rotation leading to Regaining feet.

Snowky Pokey
(Hokey Cokey)

We put our right mitten in our right mitten out,
In out, in out, we shake it all about,
We do the snowky pokey and we turn around
That's what its all about
Brrrrr the snowky Pokey,
Brrrrr the snowky pokey
Knees knock, arms hug rah rah rah

Left Mitten / Bobble Hat / Right Welly / Left Welly / Ski Goggles / Ear Muffs

Activities:

2-6m: [Yolk hold] – Turn the upright baby's right shoulder toward the caregiver, maybe with a kiss on cheek, then away and so forth. Flip Flop forwards and backwards action with kiss on head for bobble hat.
OR
Supine on a mat – move body part or both arms in and out / bend both knees up and straighten together – like a yoga type action

6-12m: As above – adding leg actions in and out
OR
Supine on a mat – as above but bringing the right arm and left leg together and out and swap.

1-2yrs: [Safety hold] – Facing peers encourage initiated actions

2-4yrs: [Safety hold] or independent - Add the paddle teaching points to the actions – scoop mittens in for example. Car they dip their own ear muffs

General/Tips: There is a lot of coordination happening, so slow the pace of the song to suit their development to allow time to organise themselves. Choice is great: ask them for an idea of what we should put in and improvise. Add some dynamic moves such as sledge right in, sledge right out and add swing dips and seat lifts to add balance practice. To build on coordination you could add a post activity of can you put your right mitten and left welly in.

Progression Trail: Propulsive actions

Food Theme (Weeks 4, 5, 6 and 7)

Notable dates: Valentines Day, Shrove Tuesday, Mardi gras, burns night, 1st day of Ramadan

Jelly On A Plate

Jelly on a plate, jelly on a plate
Wibble wobble, wibble wobble
Jelly on a plate

Sausages in a pan, sausages in a pan
Sizzle sizzle, sizzle sizzle
Sausages in a pan

Noodles on a fork, noodles on a fork
Twizzle twizzle, twizzle twizzle
Noodles on a fork

Activities:

2-6m: Assisted laying on the mat to infants comfort – very small wiggles for each food type dependent on age.

6-12m: Guided climb onto mat – tummy time to sitting – small wibbles and elective flops in for each food type

1-2yrs: Independent climb out and sitting on the mat – wibbles to the song – with elective flop into a designated place turn to hold back on to the mat at the verse end.

2-4yrs: Independent Climb out – waiting turn while song singing – forward dive to agreed point and turn to swim back at end of verse. Try Log rolls on mat for sausages while song singing or forward rolls for noodles – child's choice

General/Tips: Always allow the child to climb out independently where able and allow them to initiate the jump/flop/dive independently – ensure they understand the consequence and importance of waiting until grown up ready.

Progression Trail: Widening the gap - elective submersion.

3 Current Buns

Three current buns in a bakers shop
Round and fat with a cherry on the top
Along came xxx with a penny one day
Bought a currant bun and took it away!

Two current buns in a bakers shop
Round and fat with a cherry on the top
Along came xxx with a penny one day
Bought a currant bun and took it away!

One currant buns in a bakers shop
Round and fat with a cherry on the top
Along came xxx with a penny one day
Bought a currant bun and took it away!

Activities:

2-6m – [Forward hold] Sway side to side, turn together for 'round', bubbles for the cherry then sway again and turn the opposite direction for 'took it away'

6-12m - [Safety hold] as above but assisted rotation on the axis infant only

1-2yrs – [Side hold] as above allowing the action to be as independent as possible. Maybe try a set hold or standing on a lap and the child can turn independently.

2-4yrs – [Noodle] as above allow independent rotation on the noodle or without.

General/Tips: You can add a child's name to each verse depending on how many swimmers there are, maybe you could ask first who would like to give the penny and choose 3 ensuring there is an opportunity later for others to have a turn. You could do round arms instead if required. For took it away a child could widen the gap.

Progression Trail: Turntable rotation.

6 Fat Sausages

6 fat sausages sizzling in a pan
One went pop! And the other went bang!
Now there's 4 fat sausages sizzling in a pan

4 fat sausages sizzling in a pan
One went pop, and the other went bang!
Now there's 2 fat sausages sizzling in a pan

2 fat sausages sizzling in pan
One went pop! and the other went bang!
Now there's no fat sausages sizzling in a pan.

Activities:

2-6m – [Cradle hold] or [Feet to Tummy hold] – adding a swish side to side for pop and bang

6-12m – as above adding a flip towards parent for 'pop' and a flop back in to feet to tummy for 'bang'

1-2 yrs – [Figure of 8] with a lift for 'pop' and a drop into a cuddle for 'bang'

2-4 yrs – [Noodle] independent flip flops (assisted-guided-independent-independent without aids) – for the 'pop' and 'bang' line

General/Tips: This could be done on a mat to practise log rolls or any balance work. You could work on fine motor skills of the finger in mouth pop and a hand clap bang. My tip would be to after each verse or at the end count down together talking about starting with 6 taking 2 away and asking how many there were then. Ask them how they moved from their front to their back and can they show you. Counting in twos is an advanced skill to typical counting in 1s.

Progression Trail: Vertical rotation and regaining feet

I'm a Little Pancake

I'm a little pancake on my tummy
I'm a little pancake nice and yummy
I'm a little pancake on my tummy
Flip me up and swim to Mummy
I'm a little pancake on my back
I'm a little pancake nice and flat
I'm a little pancake on my back
Flip me up and bounce me back

Activities:

2-6m – [back float hold] – floating supine carefully rotating into a prone float [forward hold] adding bubbles.

6-12m – As above adding movement from the adult for example in widths if necessary.

1-2yrs – As above

2-4 yrs – as above holding the child's hands to give support whilst independent positioning can be achieved.

General/Tips: By adding dynamics of the adult moving the water can help support the child. The swifter the walk back the more of a wake will be created to help. Ensure you are not interfering with reflexive actions such as the Segmental rolling or righting reflexes – allow these to playout naturally for independence then try again.

Progression Trail: Floatation and regaining feet

Forest Theme (Weeks 8,9,10 and 11)

Notable dates: World Book day, British Science week, Mothers day, , National tell a Fairytale day

Hug Your Bear

Hug, hug, hug your bear
Hold them very tight
Lift them high, help them fly
Then squeeze with all your might

Activities:

2-6m [Front hold] – Nice cuddles with a bounce at the end

6-12m – As above maybe a higher jump

1-2yrs – As above

2-4 yrs – As above aiming for the child to initiate a jump or squeeze of their parent – maybe the child could lift their parent if they can stand securely in the depth.

General/Tips: Always check if the pair would like to hug and check in each time to see if their mind has changed or the height is as they like. Could be sung as a co float/swim and change the words: kick you legs and swish your arms then swim with all your might. Great for building positive relationships!

Progression Trail: Attachment – this underpins confidence to all skills

Round and Round the Garden

Round and round the garden
Like a teddy bear,
One step, two step,
Tickle you under there.
Or
Throw you in the air
We're going under there

Activities:

2-6m – [Front hold] Adult rotates 360 degrees holding baby with either tickle, bounce or bubbles for last line

6-12m – [Front hold] adult stands stationary and rotates infant 360 degrees with a tickle, a bounce or a face dip.

1-2yrs – [Front hold] as above progressing face dip to both submerging/face dipping

2-4yrs – [Front hold] as above independent rotation with either tickle, lap jump or submersion together allowing independent surfacing

General/Tips: Always ask if the child is happy to be tickled or would they prefer to tick their parent. Same for going under there or in the air. Choice is key to a greater depth of learning. It sis essential time and understanding is given to allow choice for the submersion. Ensure there are enough pauses to help the child prepare for the correct breathing time and to do it in a way where they independently submerge (maybe from a lap) and resurface. Face dips a child can visibly dip their own head if it is their choice.

Progression Trail: Turntable rotation / Strength to surface from a breath

5 Little Bears

Five little bears Heard a loud roar
One ran away
Then there were four!
Four little bears Climbing up a tree
One slid down
Then there were three!
Three little bears Deciding what to do
One fell asleep
Then there were two!
Two little bears Having lots of fun
One went home
Then there was one!
One little bear Feeling all alone
Ran to his mother
Then there were none.

Activities:

2-6m [Front hold] – Gentle actions 5. Bubbles and turn, 4. Lift up and down 3. Close cuddles or cradle 2. Giggles and bubbles with turn 1. Close cuddles encourage gripping

6-12m – [Front hold] 5. Bubbles and kicking/turning. 4. Facing the parent in the seat encourages reaching to hold onto the parent. 3. Close cuddles or cradle. 2. Giggles and bubbles 1. Close cuddles and gripping

1-2yrs – [Holding on - Seat support] 5. Bubbles and kicking whilst supported at the bar independent turn 4. Figure of 8 3. Floatation. 2. Holding caregivers fingers, caregiver twirls child around. 1 Cuddles

2-4 yrs – [Holding on - Seat support] 5. Bubbles and kicking whilst holding the bar, independent turn 4. Monkey walks at the bar or climbs up parents arm with a turn or a drop at the end. 3. Floatation 2. Turntable rotation to holding on to parent/bar 1. Widening the gap from bar to parent or Lap jump from parent to turn and hold on.

General/Tips: 5 – Kick legs for running , 4 – lift up and down for sliding down , 3 – Float practice for sleep, 2 – Rotation for going home, 1 – A hug or swim under water for run to mother. I have built on holding on throughout this song, but you could pick other trails and build on those e.g. propulsion. Great for social engagement and bonding, literacy numeracy you name it this song has it!

Progression Trail: Holding on

Teddy Bear Teddy Bear

Teddy Bear Teddy Bear Rev your boat
Teddy Bear Teddy Bear, Lay back and float

Teddy Bear Teddy Bear push the side
Teddy Bear Teddy Bear hold that glide.

Teddy bear, teddy bear, arms up high
Teddy bear, teddy bear, paint the sky

Activities:

2-6m: [Feet to tummy] for float and push adding a twirl for painting the sky.

6-12m – As above swinging them out into a back float to kick for the paint.

1-2yrs – as above encourage arms and legs for painting, more independence in the pushes and movements.

2-4yrs – [Holding on] to a wall blow bubbles then lay back looking up, gently push from the side to glide then paint a rainbow in the sky with arms. Start assisted then noddle guided, noodle independent then independent guided then independent.

General/Tips: Really popular and familiar song, try changing the verse to suit an interest i.e. dinosaurs or think of other rhymes to connect to swimming i.e. Teddy bear teddy bear reach for the trees, teddy bear teddy bear kick and paddle please. Of course there's the favourite touch the ground and turn around or wall in we fall. Big tip as always is communication and choice.

Progression Trail: Body Position – Push and Glides Supine

Spring / Easter theme (Weeks 12, 13, 14, 15, and 16)

Notable dates: Spring equinox, Easter, Eid al Fitr, Unicorn Day

I Hear Thunder

I hear thunder, I hear thunder
Hark don't you, hark don't you
Pitter patter rain drops, pitter patter rain drops
I'm wet through, so are you

Activities:

2-6m – [Front hold] Rhythmic flip flops slowing the pace down to suit (I hear thunder/hark don't you) – bobbing slowly up and down (Pitter patter and wet through)

6-12m – [Side hold] – Forwards and backwards action (I hear thunder) – figure of 8 action (hark don't you) – Turn into [Front Hold] and encourage leg kicks or bubbles (rain drops /I'm wet though)

1-2yrs – All actions are *Assisted/Guided as below*

2-4 yrs – *All actions Guided/Independent.* Monkey walking along the wall/bar hands together hands apart (I hear thunder) – Turn and point with 1 hand (Hark don't you) – Push towards and agreed point with big whoosh (pitter patter rain drops) – Long fast splashy toes (I'm wet though)

General/Tips: This could be a fantastic, coordinated rhythm – younger babies tracking the noise and watching different actions. Older joining in and cross patterning complex movements – Try this rhythm: Splash (right hand – I), Splash (Left hand - hear), Clap Clap (centre - thunder) x2 – shake hands from centre to wide apart (hark don't you) and back again (hark don't you). Finger tapping along the surface of water or one side of the body then other (Pitter patter rain drops). Wiping the face with water – (I'm wet through.). Of course if the children are really enjoying just the fun of splashing then go with it there is a lot of value in just the cause and effect of getting wet!

Progression Trail: Holding on and Widening the gap

Sleeping Bunnies

See the sleeping bunnies sleep until it's nearly noon,
Shall we go and wake them with a merry tune?
They're so still, are they ill?
Wake up soon
Hop little bunnies, hop, hop, hop.
Hop little bunnies, hop, hop, hop.
Hop, hop, hop, hop hop.

Frogs – jump, Pigs – fly, Horses – gallop, Birds – soar.

Activities:

2-6m – [Cradle hold/Back float] – Eye gazing and gentle movements after wake up soon slow rhythmic swing dips – relaxed allow baby to feel buoyancy and water on ears.

6-12m – [Back float] – Adjust positioning so legs are always relaxed in the water and that the infant is not trying to roll or get up right (we don't want to hinder these automatic reactions) – this may mean having them almost fully sat up against the parents chest. For the hop we can support to bounce or flip flop

1-2yrs – As above

2-4yrs – As above – by now the child however should feel in control and have trust with adults so we can begin to lessen our hold to 1 finger support under occiput or supported by their hands only whilst they independently get into position. Ultimately, we are aiming for full independence. The end can be regaining feet and hopping or kicking legs to make the float dynamic.

General/Tips: I love the choice in this song, try asking the children which animal and what action they think they should do for that animal. Keeps it interesting and gives opportunity for a variety of swim skills to be included alongside gross, fine motor skills and cognitive development.

Progression Trail: Back Floating

Peter Rabbit

Peter rabbits got a fly upon his nose,
Peter rabbits got a fly upon his nose
Peter rabbits got a fly upon his nose,
So he flipped it and he flopped it
and the fly flew away.
Floppy ears and curly whiskers,
floppy ears and curly whiskers,
floppy ears and curly whiskers,
So he flipped it and he flopped it
and the fly flew away.

Activities:

2-6m – [Front Hold] – bringing infant nose to nose with adult in a forward and backwards motion x3, Nose wiggles (flipped flopped flew away.) Cheek Dips (Ears and whiskers). Nose wiggles (flipped flopped flew away)

6-12m [Front Hold] – Mirroring parent to nose/face dips (fly upon his nose) and nose/face wiggle in water (flip flop), bubbles (flew away). PAUSE (to see if they copy). Cheek dips (ears and whiskers) and nose/face dip/bubbles (flip, flop, flew) PAUSE.

1-2yrs [Front Hold] – Build on above encouraging mouth closing and bubbles throughout and increasing opportunity for independence (check they are stable in hold – would they prefer their feet on a surface?)

2-4yrs – (Side Hold) – Encourage independent face dip with a turn back to adult for flew away building up to a lap jump from adult to independently turntable rotation back to hold on to adult.

General/Tips: Traditionally 'Peter Rabbit' is sung with both hands mimicking bunny ears on the head 'got a fly upon his nose' is sung pointing to the nose. One hand wafts the nose one way then the other wafts it again for 'he flipped it and he flopped it' then one last hand to waft continues flying past with an undulated action for 'the fly flew away. 'Floppy ears' – make floppy ears with hands, 'curly whiskers' twirl fingers at cheeks making the twirls get wider and further away from the face and finally back to the flip flopping waft action for the fly flew away. A great song to pace slowly to allow the children time to motor plan, coordinate the movements. Maybe ask if they would like a fly on their nose, did Peter Rabbit like the fly on his nose?

Progression Trail: Elective Submersion with turntable rotation

Wiggly Worm

Theres a worm at the bottom of the garden,
And his name is wiggly woo,
Theres a worm at the bottom of the garden,
And all that he can do,
Is wiggle all day and wiggle all night
And that's what all the people say,
Theres a worm at the bottom of the garden
And his name is wiggly woo.

Activities:

2-6m – [Back float] – 2 hand support under head / neck and shoulder (very slow gentle recline) – adult to look down to encourage baby to look up – slow backwards walk either in a circle or width organisation to avoid collisions.

6-12m [Back float] – Slowly recline watching for signs of righting or rolling reflexes – pause if notice to see if they settle and relax if not allow them to sit up or roll over and try again later. Adding movement in the form of a backward walk from the adult adding a gentle swish and keywords kick at the end of the verse. Hand support can be reduced to one hand under the head or even 1 finger for babies secure in this position.

1-2yrs [Back float] – Developmentally at this age the child is programmed to move so allow them freedom to move out of this position when they wish – go with whatever you can consensually get you will be rewarded later for listening to their needs

2-4yrs – [Back float] – Aided – starting with full assistance, gently guiding to independence. You can support, but allowing them to initiate the propulsion and correct their own body position, reduce support with consent

General/Tips: I love how the words roll off your tongue with this song. We can add lots of expression to the words and facial gestures to encourage looking up. I do like to encourage the children to regain feet and swim to the wall. Top tip would be to use your words carefully Such as SLIDE away from the wall rather than PUSH.

Progression Trail: Back Swimming

Baa baa

Baa baa black sheep have you any wool?
Yes sir, yes sir, three bags full
One for the Master, one for the Dame,
And one for the little boy who lives down the lane.
Thank you to the Master,
Thank you to the Dame
Thank you to the little boy who lives down the lane.

**Baa baa

Buzz buzz honey bee is your honey sweet?
Yes sir yes sir, good enough to eat
Honey for your warm toast and honey for your cake
Honey by the spoonful as much as I can make

Cluck, cluck, red hen, have you any eggs?
Yes sir, yes sir, as many as your legs
One for your breakfast and one for your lunch
Come back tomorrow I'll have another bunch

Activities:

2-6m – [Basic Safety hold] – gentle sways side to side, a move forward for the master and turn around for the dame and a trotting bob action for the boy down the lane. Gentle seat lift for the thank you

6-12m [Seat hold] – As above supported.

1-2 yrs [Seat hold] – As above less or no support

2-4 yrs – [Seat hold] – As above encouraging arm swishes and 3 splashes for the three bags full. Encourage face dips like bowing for the master, parent to turntable whilst the child balances or child bobs underwater like a curtsey for the dame and for the little boy they can be bobbed up and down or they can forward dive off the parents hand and swim to a designated point. They can sign 'thank you'

General/Tips: Have fun, nice rhythm, the children I find love this tune and often request it. I think it's the slow beat followed by the faster pace that is most enjoyed. Ask the children which colour sheep you should choose today.

Progression Trail: Balance

**I have added other verses you could sing working on the same progression or another thread if you chose.

Space / Transport (Weeks 17, 18, 19, 20 and 21)

Noable dates: Star wars day,

3 Little Men in a Flying Saucer

3 Little Men in a flying saucer, flew around the world one day They looked left and right,
But they didn't like the sight, So one man flew away!

2 Little Men in a flying saucer, flew around the world one day They looked left and right,
But they didn't like the sight, So one man flew away!

1 Little Men in a flying saucer, flew around the world one day He looked left and right,
But he didn't like the sight, So one man flew away!

Activities:

2-6m – [Yolk Hold] – smooth low fluid swishes side to side, dipping cheeks one way, parent also then the other way until one man flew away then all around on the spot with a cheek carefully in the water.

6-12m [Open Safety] – Smoothly chin in moving forward, keeping shoulders under the water guide onto back with ears in looking up in a flip flop action. Then for one man flew away all the way around on front rotating horizontally onto back and then on the next verse all around on the front horizontally rotating onto the front.

1-2yrs [Open Safety] – As above encouraging them start to change positions independently
2-4yrs – (Open Safety) – As above encouraging more independence for the rotation. Allow them to float at the end. Encourage independence, good body positioning i.e. ears in looking up.

General/Tips: We like to change the words to this song for example on Star Wars Week we will sing ' 3 Jedi knights in an X wing fighter flew around the galaxy one day' For Aladdin we will sing 3 humpy camels trotted through the desert one day they didn't like the sand so one camel rode away. Children tend to love big movements, however be mindful that the pace should be individual.

Progression Trail: Horizontal Rotation

Zoom Zoom Zoom

Zoom zoom zoom we are going to the moon,
Zoom zoom zoom we're going very soon,
If you want to take a trip
Climb on board my rocket ship
5, 4, 3, 2, 1,
Blast Off!

Activities:

2-6m [Back Float hold] – Start with Baby's feet on the wall (allow exploration), head on parents shoulder parent can sing and sway to the rhythm then 5, 4, 3, 2, 1 and push the wall with feet and blast off through the water and kick to the other side and repeat. We can progress this at baby's pace to them being supported with their ears in the water.

6-12m [Back Float hold] – As above may need to be supported head on shoulder and maybe need to rotate on to front after the blast off

1-2 Yrs. [Back Float hold] – As above. Ensure the child is pushing the wall with their feet and ears in the water.

2-4yrs [Back float hold] – Child attempting to hold on at the wall and leaning back looking up ready to push and glide on the 5, 4, 3, 2, 1.

General/Tips: A popular song amongst children who love the feeling of jumping and pushing. This song can be sung with the blast off being a throw up in the air which is a really fun way also. Sometimes you may find the waiting too long? If so drop the If you want to take a tip, climb on board my rocket ship lines out.

Progression Trail: Body Position - Supine Push and Glides

Big Tractor

Jumping up and down a on a big …..
Tractor
Jumping up and down a on a big …..
Tractor
Jumping up and down a on a big …..
Tractor *Bringing in the Hay, Hey!*

Activities:

2-6m [Yolk Hold] – Gentle bobs up and down to the song with the last line being a little higher!

6-12m [Seat Hold] – As above

1-2yrs [Seat/stand hold] – as above or allow child to stand on parents knees and bounce if depth allows.

2-4yrs [Standing on parents' knees or in hands] encourage arms in the air for the jump up at the end.

General/Tips: The choice is endless with this song. It is the number 1 song to be chosen in my classes and I assume a big draw is that we take turns choosing a vehicle and or a colour. Examples could be Chugging along on a 2 carriage passenger train .... Taking everyone home! Or Spinning around in a dirty cement mixer... mixing up the cement!

Progression Trail: Jumping

Twinkle Twinkle

Twinkle twinkle little star
How I wonder what you are
Up above the word so high
Like a diamond in the sky
Twinkle twinkle little star How I
wonder what you are

Activities:

2-6m – Parent Lays back (holding baby with their back to parent's chest) using 1-2 noodles – baby should be cheek to check as parent reclines then once comfortable slide baby down onto their chest. (Slide back to cheek to check when regaining feet) – help individually until everyone can get into position safely.

6-12m – as above reducing floatation aids and adding slow dynamic moves – check organisation is safe. Babies with strong righting reflexes can rest face to face with their parents.

1-2yrs – As above maybe progress to gentle co swims around a circuit or in widths – check organisation.

2-4 yrs – As above encouraging the child to assist with the sculling action needed to move. Trying to get both parent and child to have ears in the water – does the song sound different under the water?

General/Tips: When the pace of your class is a little too fast and the children are getting overloaded leading to melt downs and low concentration. Try adding this song. As the parents relax, so will the children. Adding relaxation into your groups will enhance learning. Use for co floating or swimming or use for independent floating.

Progression Trail: Co-Floatation, relaxation

The Wheels on the Bus

The wheels on the bus go round and round Round and round, round and round
The wheels on the bus go round and round All day long.
The wipers on the bus go swish swish
The horn on the bus goes beep beep
The conductor on the bus goes tickets please
The children on the bus go up and down
The babies on the bus go fast asleep (or wah wah)

Activities:

2-6m – Close holds face to face. Various actions; turning on the spot together (wheels) cheek dips (swish), gentle lift (jump up and down) cradle (fast a sleep)

6-12m – Various supportive holds with room for bigger movements. Various actions; turn infant on the spot (wheels), independent cheek dips (swish), seat hold lifts (jump up and down), Back floating (fast asleep)

1-2yr – As above allowing for less support, self initiated and more independent moves where possible

2-4 yrs – Progressing through Assisted, Guided and to independent moves. The turn could become a independent 360 (wheels) and face in with side rotation or breaststroke arms (swish), standing lifts (jump up and down) and independent floating (fast asleep)

General/Tips: Such a versatile song! Children love the repetitiveness of this delightful song. Choosing the verses will tell your children you trust their choice that they have great ideas! The wheels can be anything? Breaststroke arms? Turntable rotation, somersaults, log rolls? This is another tune that can be used for so many themes! The frogs in the pond hop up and down, the jelly fish in the sea go wiggle wiggle wiggle! The world is your oyster with this song.

Progression Trail: Jumping, rotation, propulsion

Oceans / Safety Theme (Weeks 22, 23, 24, and 25)

Notable dates: Turtle day, World Ocean day, STA Learn to swim week, RLSS Drowning prevention week, environment day, world reef day

Motorboat

Motorboat, motorboat going so slow
Motorboat, motorboat going so fast
Motorboat, motor boat step on the gas!

Activities:

2-6m – [Side hold] – chins on the water (support chin if necessary) travelling head first direction, baby held horizontally to parents side – parent takes baby around in a circle (parent turns on the spot) adjusting speed along with ensuring it is a good pace for their child – slow, faster, then faster for step on the gas adding "kick kick kick"

6-12m [Open Safety] – As above

1-2yrs [Open Safety] – As above but flipping onto back for step on the gas and kicking!

2-4yrs [Figure of 8 hold] – as above but trying for them to independently get a good body position by holding their hands only. At first parents may need to initiate the momentum, but we are aiming for independent propulsion. We could even add a widening the gap swim, to the step on the gas. If so, ensure it is elective and child initiated

General/Tips: We love this song just for the fun of it and sometimes sing it for the sensory seekers lifting the child high in the air as we twirl too. You can alter the action focus easily, i.e. adding rotation as the main focus or bubbles. I think kicking works really well as the children often want to get involved to go faster.

Progression Trail: Propulsion - Legs

Fish Alive

One, two, three, four, five
once I caught a fish alive
six, seven, eight, nine, ten
then I let it go again
Why did you let it go?
Because it bit finger so!
Which finger did it bite?
This little finger on my right!

Activities:

2-6m [Tummy time on mat] – lay baby feet to edge on tummy and parent can sing the song with gentle finger taps on baby's back to the rhythm of the song.

6-12m [Sat/laid prone on the mat] – As the child wishes and is developmentally correct for their age child to sit supported by caregiver singing the song with help to lean forward to enter the water for a cuddle and bite my finger.

1-2yrs [Sat on the Mat] – Feet to edge sat up. Singing the song together with a little shake of the mat on 5 and 10. Lots of emotive faces and on bites my finger allow the children time and space to lean forward and dive/jump to their caregiver

2-4yrs [Sat on the mat] – feet to the middle of the mat, backs to mat edge caregiver supervising – sing the song shaking on 5 and 10 as above. On bites my finger the children may decide to turn and enter as above or roll backwards into the water

General/Tips: We love to add some cross patterning exercises into this song for better body control and brain development. For example: which is your right hand, which is your little finger, can you touch your nose with that finger or your left ear? Babies could lay on the mat on their backs and you could bring their right fingers to their left toes and right toes to their left hand. Can they curl up and stretch out?

Progression Trail: Balance and Independent swims

A Pirates Life

When I was ONE I sucked my thumb,
The day I went to sea.
I jumped aboard a pirate ship,
And the captain said to me...
We're going this way that way.
Forwards, backwards, over the Irish sea
A spoonful of honey to fill my tummy!
And that's the life for me! OO ARR!
When I was TWO I buckled my shoe,
The day I went to sea.
I jumped aboard a pirate ship,
And the captain said to me ...
Chorus
When I was THREE I bashed my knee,
The day I went to sea.
I jumped aboard a pirate ship,
And the captain said to me...
Chorus
I was FOUR I knocked on the door,
The day I went to sea.
I jumped aboard a pirate ship,
And the captain said to me...
Chorus
When I was FIVE I learnt to dive
The day I went to sea
I jumped on board a pirate ship
And the captain said to me
Chorus

Activities:

2-6m – [Feet to Tummy] parent sways side to side takes step forward/backward and lifts a kiss from you is all I need lifting for a kiss

6-12m – [Figure of 8] as above, action as the words state bringing them into a float for the kiss (careful they will let go)

1-2yrs – [As above or in the little harbour] allowing them to try to initiate the actions

2-4yrs – [Catamaran] supported / guided/ independent self initiated actions

General/Tips: It's quite a lengthy song so I just sing the chorus. It can be performed by the adult holding the child and moving them. Big tip is to keep an eye on how the body feels (if facing away) and facial expressions so you know how the child is feeling and can respond accordingly.

Progression Trail: Orientation leading to back work

Tiny Tim

I have a little turtle,
his name is tiny Tim
I put him in the bathtub
to see if he could swim!
He drank up all the water,
and ate up all the soap!
Now he's sick in bed with
bubbles in his throat!
Bubbles, Bubbles, Bubbles, POP!

Activities:

2-6m – [Cradle hold] – Gently rocking baby. For the bubbles: blow bubbles down the side of baby from head to toe with big explosive bubble at the end

6-12m – [Yolk hold] – Gentle sways, bobs for drank and ate, facial expressions throughout and bubbles with a bounce in the air for pop (or face dips) or as below

1-2yrs – [Seat hold] – Actions as above or hold as above. Instructor can do sign language for child to watch

2-4yrs – [Safety hold] – Facing into a circle to watch and attempt to copy the sign language options: See Video link: https://youtu.be/ixOXXfbEhus?si=l2vbhRghrBkALAdb

General/Tips: This is a lovely coming together calm song – I find children relax and calm whilst listening and interacting with this song but also enjoy the exciting pop at the end! Sign language really piques their interest and you get lots of concentration!

Progression Trail: Orientation, Aquatic Breathing!

Summer Theme (Weeks 26, 27, 28, and 29)

Notable dates: Summer equinox, Holiday time, School holidays

Grand Old Duke of York

Oh, the grand old Duke of York
He had ten thousand men
He marched them up to the top of the hill and he marched them down again!
When they were up, they were up
And when they were down, they were down
And when they were only halfway up they were neither up nor down!

Activities:

2-6m – [Basic Safety hold] walking in a circuit or in widths; raise child on up, lower on down – keep a check to see if speed and height is acceptable for the individual

6-12m – [Seat hold] As above ensuring support is given to prevent accidental falls

1-2yrs – [Seat hold] As above with support but add seat throws ensuring safety at all times.

2-4yrs – [Standing hold] – Start this stationery CAREFULLY lots of Space checking for consent to the rises and lowering – lead to independent jumps from parents hand to turn and swim back at the end. NB: Must be CHILD LED with time given to make an independent decision to jump, submerge and turn! Skills will need to be broken down prior to ensure they are capable. Always support to the level the child would like and that is safe.

General/Tips: If you have been working on lots of horizontal work such as propulsion this works really well as it changes their orientation and it's a very energetic song. Note if including a self elected submersion ensure you have included a pause to allow the child to process and decide if to act or not.

Progression Trail: Balance and elective submersion

Horsey Horsey

Horsey Horsey don't you stop
Listen to your hooves go clippity clop
Your tails goes swish
And your wheels go around
Giddy up you homeward bound

Activities:

2-6m [Seat hold] – Full support (ensure head is supported) move across the pool in widths to the song.

6-12m [Seat hold] – Support as needed lifting up and down to comfort level of child 1 width and turn around 180 degrees and giddy up back

1-2yrs [Seahorse] – Parent and child on the horse together encourage holding on, as above

2-4yrs [Seahorse] – Child independent on the horse supported as they desire as this will be slower the turn can be 360 in the middle of the width with as fast as you can giddy up to the wall.

General/Tips: You could do a back ride activity also from 1 year up? Note to ensure parents are happy to regain feet individually before performing for the first time. Ensure everyone know which direction and safety points.

Progression Trail: Propulsion, Turntable Rotation and Balance

Ring O Roses

Ring o ring a roses
A pocket full of poses
Ah-tissue ah-tissue
We all fall down.
*Down at the bottom of the deep blue sea
Catching fishes for my tea
A one, a two, a Three.*

Activities:

2-6m [Yolk hold] – Cheek dip rotations (parent and child dips cheeks and rotate face to face 180 then dip opposite cheek and rotate back) for first 2 lines the bubbles for a tissue and fall down (leading to parent face dips), gentle bobbing for the chorus with a gently lift after 3,

6-12m As above – Leading to child independently face dipping

1-2yrs As above – leading to parent submerging on fall down

2-4 yrs As above – leading to child led submersion after 1, 2 , 3 we will pause and ask if they want to go under after the bounce (and LISTEN to their answer whether verbal or body language) then lift up and allow the child to drop in (IF THEY ARE HAPPY and its is SAFE)

General/Tips: Note always to use pauses, choice, consent, check pace. Lovely for mirroring and progressing through from parent bubbles, child bubbles, parent face dips, child face dips, parent submersion, child submersion. My biggest tip must be watch their body language here because the body always tells the truest story.

Progression Trail: Elective submersions

Green Frog

Glub, glub! Went the little green frog
one day
Glub glub! Went the little green frog
Glub, Glub went the little green frog
one day and they all went
Glub, glub, gluuuuuubbbbb.
But we know frogs go
Tralalalala, tralalala, tralalala
We know frogs go
Tralalala, they don't go
Glub, glub, gluuuuub!

Activities:

2-6m - [Yolk hold] - The adult pulls a funny face then sticks their tongue out for 'glub glub' with big raspy bubbles for 'gluuubbbbb', and gentle side to side sways for the chorus.

6-12m - [Yolk hold] - As above with the addition of parental face dips on 'gluubbb'

Option 2: Sitting on a raft feet in the water - encourage leaning forward after a signal to electively flop into the water for the first gluuuubbb

1-2yrs - [Little Harbour (face to face)] - Building on above with a pause on the second round after glub to allow for elective dips
Option 2: Sitting on a raft/or poolside - feet in the water. Allowing a forward dive on gluuuubbb

2-4yrs - [Catamaran] - As above giving space and time to pop their own face in and blow bubbles if they wish
Option 2: Sitting/Standing on a raft or poolside - Allowing jump/dive forwards to their parent on gluuuubbb and spinning around for tralalala and holding back onto the poolside/raft for the second gluuuubbb

General/Tips: Slow the song to build anticipation and experiment with the dramatisation of the gluuuubbb which do the children prefer? Allowing dramatic pauses also allows processing time needed for the child to independently plan and copy. This song can become 'flip flop' went the little green frog one day, to help with floatation and rotation. Or splish splash went the... (for confidence), Or dip dip went the... (for cheek dips). Great one that you can change with a theme. For example I use 'buzz buzz with the little bumble bee one day' in my bee themed lesson.

Progression Trail: Water Confidence – Elective submersion.

Fairy Tales (Prince and Princesses) - (Weeks 30, 31, 32, and 33)

Notable days: Yorkshire Day

Humpty Dumpty

Humpty Dumpty sat on a wall
Humpty dumpty had a great fall
All the King's horses
and all the King's men
Couldn't put humpty together again

Activities:

2-6m - [Cradle hold] - Lift to a seated position and laid position for wall and fall, then swaying for the king's men

6-12m - Sat on a mat – Assisted or guided leaning forward with consent/ self initiation - lean forward on had a great fall with bobs up and down for king's men

1-2 yrs. – Seated jumps guided or independent – progressing from mat to poolside - as above

2-4 yrs – Standing jumps assisted / independent – progressing from mat to poolside - Maybe they could jump on to straddle a noodle and seahorse around like the king's men on landing.

General/Tips: Enquire there is a pause at fall to allow the children to process what will happen and decide if they wish to do it. Options for children who dont could be a swivel entry, paarnets lifting them in, holding parents hands or ensuring parents catch them before going under. Signalling is always good to allow choice.

Progression Trail: Jumping

Hickory Dickory Dock

Hickory Dickory Dock!
The mouse ran up the clock
The clock struck ONE
The mouse ran down,
Hickory Dickory Dock!
Tick Tock, Tick Tock

Hickory Dickory Dock!
The mouse ran up the clock
The clock struck TWO
The mouse went WHOO HOO
Hickory Dickory Dock!
Tick Tock, Tick Tock

Hickory Dickory Dock!
The mouse ran up the clock
The clock struck THREE
The mouse went weeeeee
Hickory Dickory Dock!
Tick Tock, Tick Tock

Hickory Dickory Dock!
The mouse ran up the clock
The clock struck FOUR
The mouse said NO MORE!
Hickory Dickory Dock!
Tick Tock, Tick Tock

Activities:

2-6m - [Basic Safety hold] - Lifting baby up and down with the words, checking pace and height. Swaying side to side for tick tock

6-12m- [Seat hold] - as above

1-2yrs - [Seat hold] - As above trying to allow more independent balance, maybe they like higher lifts now? Can they dip their ears for tick tock?

2-4yrs - [Standing hold] - Can they balance as they are lifted - do they want to fall under or stay above when lowering? - Ensure there's a pause to choose

General/Tips: Such good fun! Ensure you have enough room to be safe from accidental knocks and that you have explained to parents before starting about lifting to their child's comfort level and happiness.

Progression Trail: Balance

3 Little Monkeys

3 Little Monkeys jumping on the bed
One fell off and bumped his head
Mummy called the doctor and the
doctor said No more monkeys
jumping on the bed.

2 Little Monkeys jumping on the bed
One fell off and bumped his head
Mummy called the doctor and the
doctor said No more monkeys
jumping on the bed.

1 Little Monkeys jumping on the bed
One fell off and bumped his head
Mummy called the doctor and the
doctor said No more monkeys
jumping on the bed

Activities:

2-6m - Tummy time on the mat - When their head control is great enough very gentle light vibrations on the mat can be made - Parents sing and interact with their baby's.

6-12m - Sat on a mat – Assisted or guided leaning forward with consent/ self initiation - lean forward on one fell off and kiss to the head for bumped his head (with consent)

1-2 yrs. – Seated jumps guided or independent – progressing from mat to poolside - as above

2-4 yrs – Standing jumps assisted / independent – progressing from mat to poolside - As above

General/Tips: this is really good for learning to take turns and wait. Even if all children fall off together if you have the space to be safe they are waiting til the appropriate time. Leaning forward is key here, take time to practise it before the song.

Progression Trail: Jumping

Three Little Fishes

Three little fishes,
see how they swim
See how they swim!
Up and down,
and around they go!
Now they are tired
and swimming slow
Three little fishes

Activities:

2-6m - [Front hold] - Slow and close side to side sways, up and down bobs and parent turns on the spot, returning to swaying.

6-12m - [Front hold] - As above pace appropriate to age and desire of the child

1-2yrs - [Figure of 8] - Sway side to side chins in the water, Flip backwards then forwards (up and down) then around in a circle on the spot (around they go) - back to side to side chins in.

2-4yrs - [Figure of 8] - As above but on their backs side to side, flip forward then backwards, then round in a circle recommencing the side to side action on backs

General/Tips: Have some rhythmic fun, make sure the child's body feels and looks happy when doing the back work. its completely fine to mix it up and return to an earlier progression. Every child is different and will have different sensations when tipping backwards and we should always listen to what they are saying both verbally and physically.

Progression Trail: Water Orientation / Back swims.

Busy Brains (Weeks 34, 35, 36, and 37)

Here is the Beehive

Here is the beehive.
But where are all the bees?
Hiding away where nobody sees.
Here they come flying out of their hive.
One, two, three, four, five!
Chorus
Buzz up high. Buzz down low.
Buzzing fast. Buzzing slow.
Buzz to the left. Buzz to the right.
Buzz all day but sleep at night

Activities:

2-12m - [Safety hold] - Actions are: hold one closed fist out in front (here is the beehive), gesture 'where' with the other hand (where are all the bees), using the 'where' hand cover up the fist (hive) for (hiding away where nobody sees), then remove that hand as you sing (here they come flying out of the hive) then lift 1 finger in turn for 1,2,3,4, and finally on 5 we have a lift into the air.

1-4yrs - [Seat hold] - Encouraging independence and copying of the actions allow the child to balance on parents hand progressing the independence as their skill and confidence improves

General/Tips: The chorus is wonderful and you could add an array of actions and independence finishing in a back float for sleep all night. The word Buzz could be mouthed high in the air, low in the water, buzzing fast/slow, swinging to left and right. Lots of annotations will really help children understand concepts of high/low/fast and slow.

Progression Trail: Balance, Aquatic breathing

Honey Bees

Three little honeybees sat on a high up tree
Eating the most delicious things,
One flew off with the swarm
Where it was nice and warm
Then there were 2 nice honey bees
Buzz Buzz
Two little honeybees sat on a high up tree.
Eating the most delicious things
One flew off with the swarm,
where it was nice and warm
Then there was one nice honeybee
Buzz buzz
One little honey bee
Sat on a high up tree
Eating the most delicious things
She flew off with the swarm
where it was nice and warm
Then there were no nice honeybees
Buzz buzz

Activities:

2-6m - [Basic Safety into Open Safety] - Get the parents down low to be cheek to cheek to their child swaying and when 1 flys away:extend their arm being sure to support babies with weak head control turn on the spot - turning them to be face to face for the buzz buzz.

6-12m - Sat on a mat – Assisted or guided leaning forward with consent/ self initiation - lean forward on one flew off with the swarm and being face to face for the buzz buzz

1-2 yrs. – Seated jumps guided or independent – progressing from mat to poolside - as above

2-4 yrs – Standing jumps assisted / independent – progressing from mat to poolside - As above working toward independent jumps and turn back to hold on.

General/Tips: As with any song that 'may' include the child's face being submerged, its important to go slow and ensure that there is enough time to process what may happen and for them to form a plan of how to execute the move or indeed if they do not wish to do it at all, time to make that known.

Progression Trail: Jumping / Duckling Dives / Turntable rotation

Head Shoulders Knees and Toes

Head, shoulders, knees, and toes,

knees and toes.
Head, shoulders, knees, and toes,

knees and toes.
And eyes and ears and mouth and nose.
Head, shoulders, knees, and toes,

knees and toes.

Activities:

2-6m [Cheek to cheek] - Parents use their spare arm, run the hand from head to shoulders to knees to toes etc. Move baby on to parents opposite shoulder for second round so both sides of body are touched equally OR
Option 2: Laid on a mat move down both sides of the body lifting the baby's knees to tummy then stretching back out for a wiggle for toes.

6-12m - As above maybe assisting baby to touch their opposite side knee/toes
1-2yrs - Sat on raft - encourage/assist child to touch their own body parts

2-4yrs - With use of buoyancy aids they can lay down to touch head and shoulders then regain feet to touch knees and toes and the remainder of the verse. After each verse spend some time asking if they can touch opposite sides of body first with right hand then with left

General/Tips: Cross patterning can be tricky to coordinate and ability may vastly differ in class. Do not force it with anyone who doesn't enjoy it or seems to struggle with it - instead you could try touching fingers together in the middle or hand to toes on the same side.

Progression Trail: Body awareness, cross patterning

Three Green Bottles

Three green bottles hanging on the wall,
Three green bottles hanging on the wall,
And if one green bottle should accidentally fall,
There'll be Two green bottles hanging on the wall.

Two green bottles hanging on the wall,
Two green bottles hanging on the wall,
And if one green bottle should accidentally fall,
There'll be one green bottles hanging on the wall.

Activities:

2-6m - [Cheek to cheek] - holding their hands and swaying.

6-12m -[Basic Safety hold] - Encourage hands to grip the wall and on 'fall' pause and use a signal to ask them to initiate a turn to their parent (who is blowing bubbles) with some gentle bounces once received by the parent.

1-2yrs - [Seat hold] - with as much support as required the same as above aiming for more independence and maybe some bubbles or face dips with the turn.

2-4yrs - [Seat hold / or independent] - As above aiming to get a push and glide face in, maybe even a short unaided swim once they are skill ready and confident.

General/Tips: This is a well known song and parents will know it which always helps with integrating songs into class. I never do more than 5 Green bottles as I find it can become a little too repetitive. You could add 3 hand to hand moves along the wall then 2 the 1 as the song goes? A great one for the older children is to adapt the song to be 3 Green Bottles rolling on the mat (and if one green bottle should accidentally splat!) and practise horizontal rotation.

Progression Trail: Holding on, turntable rotation, widening the gap

Autumn - (Weeks 38, 39, 40, 41 and 42)

Notable days: Autumn begins

Orange, Yellow, Red and Brown
(Head Shoulders knees and toes)

Orange, yellow, red and brown
Red and brown
Orange, yellow, red and brown
Red and brown
The autumn leaves are twirling
to the ground
Orange, yellow, red and brown
Red and brown

Activities:

2-6m - [Yolk hold] - Parent to turn on the spot at appropriate time, rhythmically sways forward and backwards at other times

6-12m - [Basic Safety hold] - Extending the arm that is supporting the child's chest into the open safety hold to rotate in a circle at the appropriate time.

1-2yrs [Forward hold] - Turning child on spot trying to allow them to initiate the action.

2-4yrs [Lap Jump/turns] Progress from allowing them to independently turn while standing on your lap/floor/platform to jumping forwards then turning to swim back.

General/Tips: This has a beautiful tune. The children may enjoy it but not the jumping in to turn independently so ensure that there is consent and enough time given from the to understand and plan the action.

Progression Trail: Turntable rotation / treading water

Dingle Dangle

When all the cows are sleeping,
and the sun has gone to bed!
UP jumped the scarecrow
and this is what he said...
*I'm a dingle dangle scarecrow
with a flippy floppy head!
I can shake my hands like this,
I can shake my feet like that.*

When all the hens are roosting
and the moons behind a cloud,
UP jumped the scarecrow
and shouted very LOUD
Chorus

When the dogs were in the kennels
and the doves were in the loft
UP jumped the scarecrow
and whispered very soft...
Chorus

Activities:

2-6m - [Cradle hold] - Gently and slowly recline baby into a floating position and with lots of facial expressions and smiles sing the song until 'up jumps' pausing at the words while we say are you ready? And swing dip them rhythmically for the rest of the verse

6-12m - [Cheek to Cheek] - As above however, sitting them upright rather than swing dips then moving side to side and encouraging hands and feet splashing.

1-2yrs - As above - encouraging self initiated sitting up on cue.

2-4yrs - [Back Float hold] - Starting with as much support as desired aiming to progress to just holding their hands for the flotation section and regaining feet (or even fully independent) - lots of splashing to finish!

General/Tips: the short duration of the floating is predictable and well tolerated so this is an amazing opportunity to get some flotation practice in. I really like to build independence of movement into this such as allowing them to make that connection of lifting their head makes their legs sink. Pause between verses and ask 'Did anyone manage to do that all by themselves?' ' Did the parents pause long enough to allow the child to try before helping?

Progression Trail: Floatation and regaining Feet

Row Row

Row, row, row your boat
gently down the stream
Merrily, merrily, merrily, merrily
life is but a dream

Row, row, row your boat
gently down the stream
And if you see a crocodile
don't forget to scream

Row, row, row your boat
Past the Autumn trees
And if you see a squirrel
Kick and paddle please

Crunch crunch crunch the leaves
Fallen on the ground
Be careful of the hedgehog
Curled up nice and round.

Activities:

2-6m [Feet to Tummy] - As we eye gaze we will slowly and rhythmically rock the baby side to side with the tune - and instead of kick and paddle please we could say blow your bubbles please, and for the hedgehog bring them in for a cuddle.

6-12m - [Front hold] as above.

1-2yrs - [Little Harbour] - As above. Aiming for self initiated rocking using head and legs to tip forwards and backwards.

2-4yrs - [Catamaran] - As above.

General/Tips: You can create so many wonderful verses to this very popular tune. I have listed 2 of the standard verses here along with two I have made up, to fit with the theme and learning outcomes. Actions to this versatile song don't need to be performed in the water, they could also be carried out on a play mat and maybe jump / roll / fall backwards into the pool from the mat as part of the actions. For example; Roll roll roll along, turning on the floor, and if it feels really fun, jump and do some more.

Progression Trail: Regaining feet, Propulsive actions

3 Little Pumpkins in a Pumpkin Patch
(3 little men in a flying saucer)

Three little pumpkins
rolled around the patch one day
They rolled all around,
but they didn't like the ground
So one pumpkin rolled away...
Two little pumpkins
rolled around the patch one day
They rolled all around,
but they didn't like the ground
So one pumpkin rolled away
One little pumpkin
rolled around the patch one day
It rolled all around,
but It didn't like the ground
So one pumpkin rolled away ...

Activities:

2-6m - [Basic Safety hold into cheek to cheek] - With the group moving in a circle, baby and adult facing forwards, once they get to a set point they roll keeping babies body tight to their chest on to their backs (adults leaning back, but feet on the floor) and walk backward until at said point again then rotate again. Pause after first round and give corrections and progressions

6-12m - [As above]

1-2yrs [As above] Progressing from the side hold into the cheek to cheek hold.

2-4yrs [On a Raft] Encouraging the children to log roll independently along the mat or in the water with a noodle allowing them to swim in widths and rotate independently.

General/Tips: Great seasonal song that I have adapted from the popular three little men in a flying saucer! Be steady with the young ones and ensure they feel the right level of containment from their caregiver to feel secure and that any child is always given the option to get back into a position that is comfortable for them. This is a great practice that will lead to independent breathing and aid front crawl later in their journey.

Progression Trail: Horizontal rotation

Autumn Leaves
(London Bridge)

Autumn leaves are falling down,
falling down, falling down
Autumn leaves are falling down,
falling on the ground
Take a rake and rake them up,
rake them up, rake them up
Take a rake and rake them up,
rake them on the ground
Make a pile and jump right in,
jump right in, jump right in,
Make a pile and jump right in,
Jump onto the ground

Activities:

2-6m - [Side hold] - Nice and close ensuring heads are supported where necessary. Move around the pool looking at the Leafs/balls in the pool - allow the baby time to track the balls, keeping the objects as still as possible.

6-12m - As above allowing reaching

1-2yrs - [Little Harbour] - Toddlers to collect the equipment to a bucket that is on a raft . Then climb on to the raft and with a seated jump jump back in to collect another. Pause after first round for progressions and corrections, use this time to encourage and praise kicking and reaching/paddling

2-4 yrs - As above but with buoyancy aids or independent pushes from A to B.

General/Tips: Go at their pace, demonstrate good technique always, even if they are too young to copy exactly as the information is still being stored. Lots of praise and they'll soon love to kick and paddle independently.

Progression Trail: Propulsion

Celebrate themes (Weeks 43, 44, 45, and 46)

Notable dates: Halloween, Guy Fawks night, remembrance Sunday, Kindness day

Can You Wiggle Like a Worm
(Do your ears hang low)

Can you wiggle like a worm?
Can you squiggle, can you squirm?
Can you crawl on the ground?
Like a beetle that is round?
Can you move with me?

Can you flip can you flop
Can you give a little hop
Can you slither like a snake?
Can you give a little shake?
Can you move with me?

Activities:

2-6m - [Yolk hold] - Moving in circuits or widths, gently wiggling side to side for the first verse and up and down for the second

6-12m - As above or in the Side hold

1-2 yrs - As above or in the Little Harbour hold

2-4 yrs - As above or with floatation aids aiming for a good front paddle actions whilst swimming to the verses with a pause after each verse to allow for teaching points to help with technique i.e. Can you show me how you'd crawl your arms nice and long? Can you squiggle and squirm your legs really fast etc Come on move with me!

General/Tips: By asking them to interpret the action we can get a good understanding of where their understanding lays and build on that. This song is great to help children have a go who ordinarily wouldn't be comfortable to try.

Progression Trail: Propulsion

There's a Spider.

There's a spider on the floor,

on the floor

There's a spider on the floor,

on the floor

There's a spider on the floor,

Tell me, are there any more?

There's a spider on the floor,

on the floor

There's a spider on my arm,

on my arm

There's a spider on my arm,

on my arm

There's a spider on my arm,

but it wont do any harm

There's a spider on my arm,

on my arm

Activities:

2-6m [Cheek to cheek] - Parents use their spare arm, gently patter their fingers along the relevant body part or in the water alongside the body. Move the baby on to the parents opposite shoulder for the second round so both sides of the body are touched equally.

6-12m - As above

1-2yrs - As above

2-4 yrs - As above - maybe the child wants to do the spider in their parent? Have some time to make some verses up such as on my toes and it jumped on to my nose - Chin let's put it in the bin?

General/Tips: Be mindful that some children may not like spiders in which case you could change the word to theirs a fairy or a lady bird. Ensure we are respectful of the children who do not wish for the spider to be on them.

Progression Trail: Body Awareness

I Have a Little Spider

I have a little spider
I'm very fond of him!
He jumps on to my shoulder
And then onto my chin
He runs down my arm
and then down my leg
he's a very sleepy spider
so I put him up to bed.
Spider... Spider...Spider WEB

Activities:

2-6m [Branch hold] - ensuring the baby's face is out of the water we can use our spare hand to be the spider. With seat lifts for spider spider web.

6-12m - [Cheek to cheek] - attempting to help the baby lay comfortably as flat as possible. Then use spare hand for the actions - jumping into a seated position and bouncing up into the air for 'Web'

1-2yrs - As above

2-4 yrs - As above progressing to floating on their backs with minimal or no support.

General/Tips: To the tune of tiny tim this lovely song is beautiful for bonding.

Progression Trail: Body positioning

Bonfire Night in the Garden

We'll be careful to stand right back
Stand right back, stand right back
We'll be careful to stand right back
On bonfire night in the garden

The fireworks will all whizz and bang
Whizz and bang, whizz and bang,
The fireworks will all whizz and bang
On bonfire night in the garden

We will shake our sparklers with our arms outstretched, arm outstretched, arms outstretched
We'll shake our sparklers with our arms outstretched,
on bonfire night in the garden

Activities:

2-6m - [Basic Safety hold] - Walking in a circle swaying forwards and backwards for the first verse, up and down for the second. Opening the hold into open safety and back in for the last

6-12m [Basic Safety hold] - turning them into flip flops (shoulders under the water nice and steady) for the first verse then as above

1-2yrs - As above

2-4 yrs - As above - Allow the child to initiate the movements where possible so that they get the connection with how their body moves.

General/Tips: This is a great seasonal song and children in my class's favourite verse is the fizz and bang. We sometimes blow bubbles than a dramatic splash to make their parents jump. Really good message about fire safety too.

Progression Trail: Water confidence

Spooky Dooky
(to the tune of Hokey cokey)
We put our right bones in our right bones out
In out, in out, we rattle them all about
We do the spooky dooky and we turn around
That's what it's all about
OOOOOOOOO - The spooky Dooky
OOOOOOOOO - The spooky Dooky
Knees bent, arms stretched. Ra Ra Ra

We put out wolf ears in, our wolf ears out
In out, in out, we shake them all about
We do the spooky dooky and we turn around
That's what it's all about
AWHOOOO - The spooky dooky
AWHOOOO - The spooky dooky
Knees Bent arms stretched, RA RA RA

Activities:

2-6m: [Front hold] – Turn the upright baby's right shoulder toward the caregiver, maybe with a kiss on cheek, then away and so forth. Cheek Dips side to side for wolf ears, and gentle rock back n forth for the pointy hat

6-12m: [Safety hold] - As above but facing peers in a circle

1-2yrs: [Safety hold] – Facing peers encourage initiated actions

2-4yrs: [Safety hold] or independent - Add the paddle teaching points to the actions – for example Scoop your bones back, long stretches.

General/Tips: Who doesn't love the hokey cokey! This again is a versatile song for different themes, just see our winter version earlier. Children love the repetition of the actions

Progression Trail: Propulsion Arms

Strange Worlds Theme (Weeks 47, 48, 49, and 50)

Notable dates: First day of advent

See the Caterpillar
(Mary had a little lamb)

See the caterpillar hump along,
hump along, hump along
See the caterpillar hump along,
out to see the world
Now the caterpillar goes to sleep
goes to sleep, goes to sleep
Now the caterpillar goes to sleep
in his warm cocoon
Soon you'll be a butterfly,
butterfly, butterfly
Soon you'll be a butterfly,
out to see the world.

Activities:

2-6m [Yolk hold] Travelling in a line or circuit for each verse. - Gentle undulation for hump, [Back float Hold] - travel in back float for sleep. [Yolk Hold] - side to side for butterfly

6-12m - [Yolk hold] Travelling in a line or circuit for each verse. - Gentle undulation for hump, [Back float hold] - travel in back float for sleep. [Yolk hold] - side to side for butterfly

1-2yrs - [Open Safety hold] - rotating on the spot undulating gently in prone (hump), change direction smooth in supine (sleep), change direction high lifts into the air (butterfly)

2-4 yrs - As above or in Little Harbour - initiating actions as independently as possible including a double arm action for butterfly

General/Tips: This is great to give body awareness - just how do you imitate a caterpillar hump? There's lots of cognition happening to organise this in the body. Children enjoy the autonomy in this one.

Progression Trail: Dolphin kick, body position

Bouncing up and down
(3 little Men in a Flying Saucer)

Bouncing up and down on a big
(colour) Rocket
Bouncing up and down on a big xxx
rocket
Bouncing up and down on a big xxx
rocket
Bouncing up and down on a big xxx
rocket
Zooming off to space! Ace!

Twirling around in a flying saucer
Twirling around in a flying saucer
Twirling around in a flying saucer

Activities:

2-6m [Seat hold] - Ensure head is fully supported, check the pace and rhythmic bounces are suitable for the individual. Add parent turning on the spot slowly for twirling and bringing them into a [basic safety] for bubbles for babbling

6-12m [Seat hold] - Support as required bobbing for bouncing, adult to move turning on the spot slowly for twirling and bringing them into a [Basic Safety] for bubbles for babbling

1-2yrs [Seat hold] - Support as required bobbing for bouncing, adult to move turning on the spot slowly for twirling and then moving forwards whilst blowing bubbles (always check safety)

2-4 yrs As above or independently with buoyancy aids. Adding an elective swim away from the parent at the very end of the verses if the child elects to do so.

General/Tips: This song comes with a warning! You will be asked for it every lesson forever!

Progression Trail: Jumping, turntable rotation and elective submersions

5 Little Sea Creatures

Five little sea creatures on the ocean floor
The shark kicked away,
now there are four!
Four little sea creatures living in the sea
The octopus paddled off,
now there are three!
Three little sea creatures wondering what
to do?
'Goodbye' said the stingray
now there are Two
Two little sea creatures having lots of fun
Off jumped the dolphin
now there is one!
One little sea creature sitting all alone
His friends came back and they all went
home

Activities:

2-6m - [Basic Safety hold] - Doing actions appropriate to the verse; kicking, paddling, waving, bouncing

6m -2 yrs - [Seat hold] -Doing actions appropriate to the verse; kicking, paddling, waving, bouncing

2-4yrs - [Seat hold / Standing in parents lap] - as above encouraging jumping off into the water for the dolphins and or friends coming home. Giving good teaching points for the actions and how to be successful in the jumps off.

General/Tips: Time taken explaining how we do something to make it work better is important here, so explain each verse in turn giving points then practise it, before moving on to the next verse. Then sing the song all in one go, with enough pauses for the children to understand, process and execute the actions independently

Progression Trail: Widening the gap – independent swimming

Down in the Jungle

Down in the jungle where nobody goes
I saw an elephant washing his clothes
With a bubbles here and bubbles there
That's the way an elephant washes his clothes

Diddly-ay, tai, a-boogie-woogie-woogie
Diddly-ay, tai, a-boogie-woogie-woogie
Diddly-ay, tai, a-boogie-woogie-woogie
That's the way an elephant washes his clothes

I saw a crocodile washing his clothes
With a snap snap here and snap snap there
I saw a snake washing his clothes
With a slither here and a slither there
I saw a monkey washing his clothes
With a Dingle dangle here and a dingle dangle there
I saw lion washing his clothes
With a roar here and a roar there

Activities:

2-6m [Yolk hold] - actions appropriate to the verse, such as swishes, sways, bubbles, bounces and for the chorus we can turn in a circle happily and jolly.

6m - 2 years [Safety hold] - actions appropriate to the verse, such as swishes, sways, bubbles, bounces and for the chorus we can turn in a circle happily and jolly. Encourage copying.

2-4yrs [Aided] encouraging imitation and interpretation of actions

General/Tips: Lovely for Unique self and having a bit of fun. Allowing them to voice will say I trust you and will build self-esteem and help with their decision-making process. Great song!

Progression Trail: Water confidence and propulsion - arms

If You're a Dinosaur
(Happy and you know it)

If you're a T-rex and you know it
show your claws
If you're a t-rex and you know it
show your claws
If you're a t-rex and you know it
and you really want to show it
If you're a t-rex and you know it
show your claws.

If you're an Ankylosaurus, and you know it,
swish your tail
If you're an Ankylosaurus, and you know it,
swish your tail
If you're an Ankylosaurus
and you really want to show it

Activities:

2-12m [Safety hold] - Demonstrating, encouraging actions, appropriate actions to the verse.

1-2yrs [Little Harbour] - Encourage actions and moves appropriate to verse

2-4yrs [As above or aided] - Encourage actions and moves appropriate to verse. Allow them to choose the dinosaur (even if the answer is a cow!) and the action.

General/Tips: Lovely for a bit of dramatics and allowing them to express themselves or show any knowledge.

Progression Trail: Water confidence

Christmas Theme (part of winter) Weeks 51-52

Santa Got Stuck Up The Chimney

When Santa got stuck up the chimney
He began to shout, you girls and boys
Won't get any toys, If you don't let me out!
My beard is black!
I've got soot in my sack!
And my nose is tickling too!
When Santa got stuck up the chimney
Achoo achoo achoo!

Activities:

2-6m – [Yolk hold] – Expressive faces – Mirroring and Bubbles

6-12m - Sat on a mat – Assisted or guided leans forward with consent/ self initiation

1-2 yrs. – Seated jumps guided or independent – progressing from mat to poolside.

2-4 yrs – Standing jumps assisted / independent – progressing from mat to poolside

General Notes: with wagging fingers for girls and boys won't get any toys if you don't let me out. Rub pretend facial beard, point to the sack on your back, tickle nose with funny facial expressions throw or jump in to the air for up the chimney and sneeze into the water making bubbles

Progression: Jumping

Christmas Cracker
(Frere Jacque)
Christmas Cracker, Christmas cracker
In your hand, in your hand
Hurry up and pull it, hurry up and pull it
It goes BANG, It goes BANG!

Activities:

All: (First 2 lines) Rhythmic Splashes / sways / paddles / kicks / Bubbles / curl un curl hand / Figure of 8
(3rd Line) Flip Flop prone (hurry up) supine (pull it) / Arm action paddle/crawl/breast, (4th Verse) Bounce / One big splash / lap jump (on Bang).

6-12m - Sat on a mat – Assisted or guided leans forward with consent/ self initiation

1-2 yrs. – Seated jumps guided or independent – progressing from mat to poolside.

2-4 yrs – Standing jumps assisted / independent – progressing from mat to poolside

General: As above

Progression Trail: Jumping

Other celebration dates or ideas

Food Topics:
- Birthday tea
- Big night out/in
- National sausage day
- Pizza day
- National Egg day

Forest Topics:
- International day of forests.
- National hug a tree day

Space/Transport Topics:
- First moon landing celebration,
- National road safety week.
- National science week

Fairytale Topics:
- National tell a fairytale day,
- National play day,
- Unicorn day

Brainy Topics:
- National Maths week,
- National science weeks,
- Mental health week,
- National bee week

Autumn theme:
- National hug a tree day.
- National hedgehog day

Celebration Topics:
- Diwali,
- Chinese New Year,
- Birthdays,
- Australia day,
- Independence day

Other World Topics:
- Day of the dinosaurs,
- National rainbow day

Songs and Rhymes Ending Notes

I hope you have enjoyed the songs chosen for this book and that your swimmers enjoy them as much as mine do. Feel free to have a play around with words or make your own songs up after all the pen is mightier than the sword and words have power! I find songs like Row Row and Frere Jacque are amazing and simple to amend to suit various themes and skills.

A big overall tip from me is to feel into the energetics of the songs, what are the children enjoying? Are their caregivers sleepy and need a revitaliser? Or would it be more appropriate to lower the tone? Do the caregivers know the time/song and feel comfortable singing along and joining in with the actions? Do you like the song? This will all feed through into the overall energy and ultimate enjoyment in the class.

The holds and moves are suggestions only please always support the children on an individual basis to ensure they have a base of support that they are comfortable with. It's equally important to ensure that the parent is comfortable with the hold and in their stance. Take this time to ensure comfort and you'll be rewarded in a happier class!

You will see that i have included notable dates for each section these are the dates happening in the national calendars that fit in with my chosen these typically during those weeks of the year for example talk like a pirate day is typically around 19th September   here is a list of other notable days that didn't fit in with my specific themes or within the dates that i have suggested to run the theme. I have not included actual dates as these will change from year to year

Finally, communication! Communication! Communication! I mean with all of your senses

Glossary of Holds

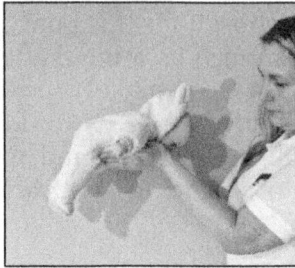

Yolk hold

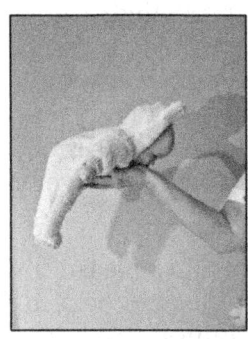

Forward Surf hold

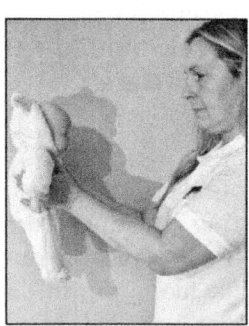

Front hold

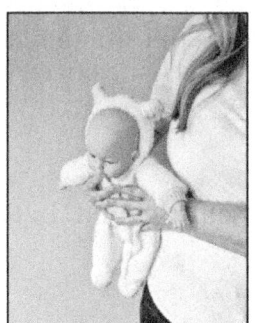

Side hold

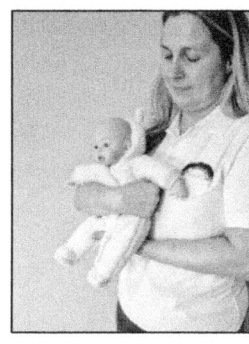 Basic Safety hold

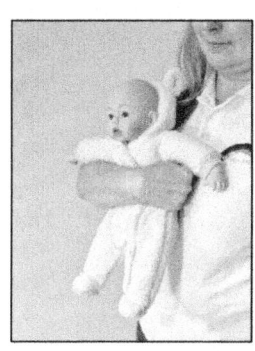 Safety hold

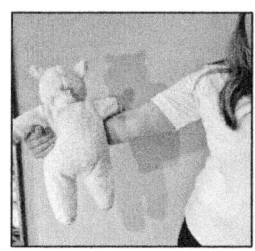 Open Safety hold

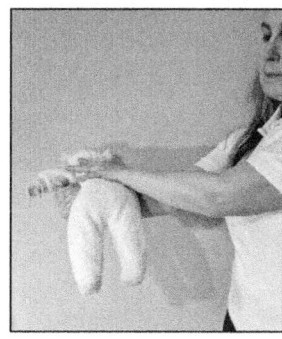 Flip flop

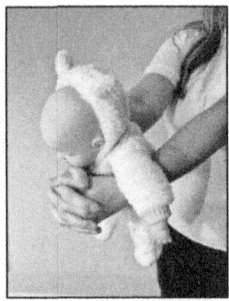 Little Harbour hold (closed)

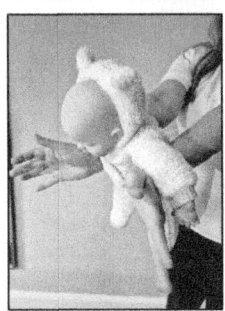 Little Harbour hold (open)

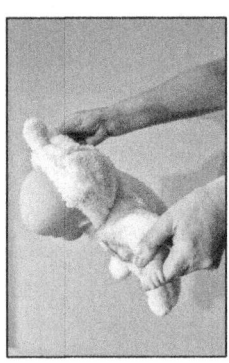 Figure of 8

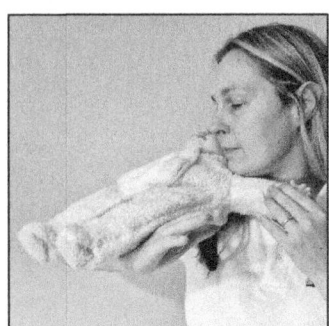 Cheek to cheek

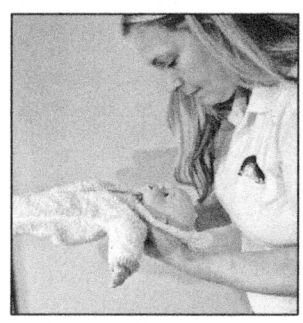 Back Float hold

 Feet to Tummy hold

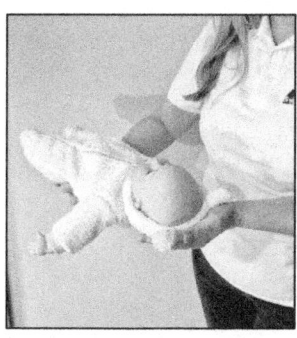 Cradle Hold

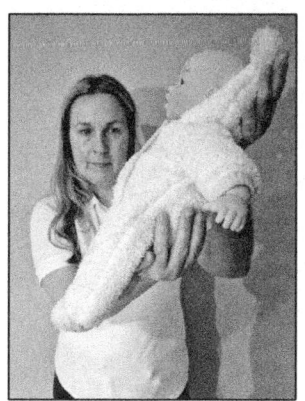 Swing Dip move

 Seated hold (supported)

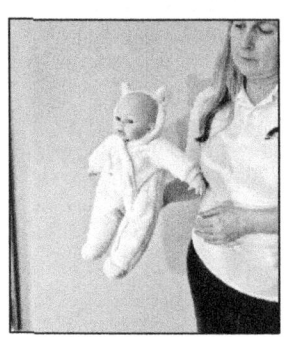 Seated hold (un supported)

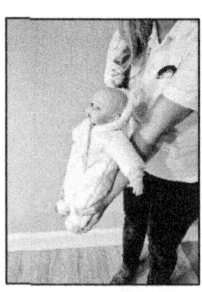 Standing hold

 Branch hold

Index
Swim Skill Progression

Attachment
    Pages 61
Balance
    Pages 47, 77, 91, 97, 99, 107, 113
Body Awareness
    Pages 117, 133, 141
Breathing
    Pages 95, 113
Co Swimming
    Pages 85
Elective Submersion
    Pages 53, 73, 97, 101, 103, 115, 143
Floatation
    Pages 59, 71, 123, 135
Holding On
    Pages 55, 69, 119
Independence
    Pages 91, 145
Jumping In
    Pages 83, 87, 105, 109, 115, 143, 151, 153
Propulsion
    Pages 51, 75, 87, 89, 99, 111, 125, 129, 131, 139, 141, 147
Push and Glides
    Pages 67, 81,
Regaining Feet
    Pages 49, 57, 59, 123, 125
Rotation - Horizontal
    Pages 79, 87, 127,
Rotation - Turntable
    Pages 47, 49, 55, 63, 73, 87, 99, 115, 119, 121, 143
Rotation - Vertical
    Pages 49, 57, 87
Surfacing to Breath
    Pages 63
Treading Water
    Pages 121,
Water Orientation
    Pages 93, 95, 103, 111, 137, 147, 149
Widening the Gap
    Pages 53, 69, 119, 145

References / bibliogr aphy List

#1 https://www.britannica.com/art/nursery-rhyme (accessed 24/10/2023)

#2 https://en.wikipedia.org/wiki/Nursery_rhyme#:~:text=The%20Roman%20nurses'%20lullaby%2C%20%22,be%20the%20oldest%20to%20survive. (accessed 24/10/2023)

#3 https://www.historic-uk.com/CultureUK/Nursery-Rhymes/ (accessed 24/10/2023)

#4 https://www.slq.qld.gov.au/blog/moving-child-learning-child (accessed 24/10/2023)

#5 https://early-education.org.uk/wp-content/uploads/2021/12/Musical-Development-Matters-ONLINE.pdf (accessed 24/10/2023)

#6 https://fagottobooks.gr/blog/music-education-sayings-and-quotes/#:~:text=%E2%80%9CMusic%20is%20a%20more%20potent%20instrument%20than%20any%20other%20for%20education.&text=%E2%80%9CMusic%20education%20stimulates%2C%20challenges%2C,its%20value%20lasts%20a%20lifetime.&text=%E2%80%9CWe%20need%20highly%20skilled%20workers%20to%20think%20and%20create. (accessed 24/10/2023)

#7 https://www.savethemusic.org/resources/advocacy-tools/music-ed-quotes/ (accessed 24/10/2023)

#8 https://www.nidcd.nih.gov/health/speech-and-language#:~:text=The%20first%203%20years%20of,speech%20and%20language%20of%20others. (accessed 24/10/2023)

#9 - https://www.ncbi.nlm.nih.gov/pmc/articles/PMC4166894/ (accessed 24/10/2023)

#10 https://www.dvusd.org/cms/lib/AZ01901092/Centricity/Domain/3795/Sound_Spelling_Chart.pdf (accessed 24/10/2023)

#11- https://funmusicco.com/how-does-music-stimulate-left-and-right-brain-function-and-why-is-this-important-in-music-teaching/ (accessed 24/10/2023)

Bowlby, J. (1969) *Attachment and Loss: Volume 1. Attachment*, New York, Basic Books

Mate, G (2019), Scattered Minds, Ebury Publishing

Blomberg, H (2011), Movements that Heal, edition 1, BookPal, Queensland Australia

Seuss, (2005), Happy Birthday to you, Harper Collins Children's Books, USA

Burgam, K, Et Al (2016) STA Level 3 Diploma in Aquatic teaching – Baby and preschool, Swim Teachers Association, Walsall

Montessori, M (2009), An Absorbent Mind, BN Publishing New York

Dahlitz, M (2017), The Psychotherapists Essential Guide to the Brain, Dahliz Media, USA

Pittman, C (2015), Rewire your Anxious Brain, Wetware Media

Baxter, S (2022), Vagus Nerve Exercises to Rewire your Brain, Susan Baxter Centre of Excellence, Play therapy audio course

I Too Love Song and Rhyme

I see you with the wide grin,
I hear the giggle from within
I too love to join in and sing

I watch you move around with glee
I feel the ripples land on me
I too love to dance you see

I listen to the joyous sound
The rhythm makes my heart pound
I too love to move around

I see you splash n move in time
I hear you sing the funny line
I too love song and rhyme

By Emma Holden

Thank you for buying my book